GRANNY'S MUFFIN HOUSE

FOR SALE
12 MUFFINS &
THIS COW

BY SUSAN ASHBY
WITH AN INTRODUCTION BY
RENNY DARLING

Published by Royal House Publishing Co.
Book Division
Recipes-of-the-Month Club
P.O. Box 5027
Beverly Hills, CA 90210
Printed in the United States of America
ISBN: 0-930440-18-8

The Contents

Foreword

February 22, 1983

Dear Friends;

I love muffins. They are delightful, versatile and always fun to serve. There is something about these light and fragrant little breads that always summons up fond remembrances of pure delight.

Muffins are amazingly versatile. They can be served for breakfast, brunch, lunch or dinner. They serve well for mid-morning coffees or afternoon snacks. They are grand accompaniments to soups or salads. Served warm, with sweet, creamy butter, melting into each one of its little pores, is the stuff memories are made of.

Muffins can be sweet or savory and the number of combinations are literally endless. They can be sparkled with an infinite variety of flavors . . . fruits and berries (fresh, frozen or dried), dates, figs, nuts, vegetables, cheese, herbs and spices, all can be used to produce fine muffins. And of course, there is always CHOCOLATE. Chocolate with bananas, chocolate with dates, chocolate fudge and chocolate chips, will please the most ardent chocolate lover.

Muffins can be fashioned to serve on special holidays . . . Christmas, Thanksgiving, Easter, St. Patrick's Day . . . the list goes on and on.

Muffins are perfect for busy schedules, for they take just moments to prepare. And especially nice is that they need only to be stirred (the less, the better), so they can be prepared by the most novice cook.

Freshly baked, muffins are marvelous. But, as an extra bonus, they freeze exceedingly well. So, an extra batch or two can always await you in the freezer.

And that is why I am pleased to introduce you to "Granny's Muffin House" where many pleasures await you. Here you will find muffins to please every taste, every mood. Here you will find muffins made, not only with the traditional flour, but with whole wheat, bran, buckwheat and oatmeal. Within its tempting pages, you will find muffins, muffins and more muffins, to keep your family and friends happy for years and years.

Why not start a tradition at your home and plan special muffins for special holidays? The chapters are conveniently divided into seasons, so it will be easy to choose the fruits or vegetables that are plentiful during that time of year.

So, welcome to Toadvine, and Granny's neighbors and kin. Susan Ashby has woven a charming folk tale that will delight you. Her muffins are marvelous.

As always, enjoy with love,

Renny Darling

Renny Darling
Beverly Hills, CA

Introduction

Well, I mind it was some 70 years ago when I was a young 'un in my Granny's kitchen back in Alabamy. It was in the winter of 1913 in fact, and the wind was gettin' up mighty high, while through the windows, the snowflakes were whirlin' faster than fairies against the darkenin' sky.

"When I grow up Granny," says I, "I am going to put your muffins in a cookbook." My Granny, she jest laughed and said folks would rather have your Duck a l'Orange and your Crepes Suzettes than homegrown muffins. But my gol, now I see the humble muffin everywhere, and muffin shops sproutin' up faster than corn in the July heatwave.

Now don't get me wrong, I don't hold any grudge against your boughten muffins. But I think you should try your hand at my Granny's recipes.

Jest so's you get headed off to a good start, here's some tips to remember at all times when you're bakin' up muffins.

1 — Don't overbeat the batter or the gluten will develop and form your holes and your tunnels. Jest mix 'til dry ingredients are moistened.

2 — If the oven heat is set too high, the muffin heads above the rims of the cups will be cracked and hard.

3 — Too low an oven heat will produce peaks and hollows.

4 — If you prefer your smaller style muffins, it's best to jest fill 'er up two-thirds full, instead of the generous measure given in the book. This also applies if your muffin tins are large.

5 — Always remember, muffins are at their best the day they are baked, but if they are frozen straight away, they will be as fresh as a daisy whenever you need them. So if you make too many, don't let them set around too long.

And now that you are ready to get started, I wish you good eatin' and good times with your new found muffins.

To Granny

Spring

Now that the birds are peepin' and the trees are turnin' green, seem's like as good a time as any to take advantage of your natural world.

Round about this time every year, Granny would always send the menfolk out to gather honey for her honey-sweetened muffins. One year, Grandpa and my daddy, who was jest a little slip of a tad then, were out at that neck of the woods where the honey flows the sweetest. And who should be watchin' hard by, but a mean old mama she-bear. Soon's my Grandpa notices, he hitches my daddy up on his shoulders, and races faster than lightenin' for home.

Seem's safer to me to get your honey from your supermarket.

Mind you, when the weather's so nice, and folks all round have the spring fever, your muffins can be mighty nice for an outdoor breakfast, before you get diggin' the garden for another year's harvest.

Raisin Muffins

I mind it was last April when I made these Raisin Muffins. I'd jest come home after a harrowin' trip back from the village. It's not too bad when the dry season's on, but my gol, when the rains come and the swamp waters flood over, you have to fight all the time, jest to keep them water moccasins out of the way. Anyhow, I had a passel of raisins I'd jest bought, so I thought I'd revive myself with a batch of fresh muffins and a pot of tea.

2	**cups flour**
1	**tablespoon bakin' powder**
1/2	**teaspoon salt**
1/2	**cup sugar**
1	**egg, beaten**
1/3	**cup butter, melted**
1/2	**cup milk**
1/2	**cup sour cream**
2	**tablespoons grated lemon**
1 1/2	**cups raisins**

Preheat your oven to 400°.

Sift the first 4 ingredients together.

Stir in the egg, butter, milk and sour cream, jest till moistened.

Fold in the lemon and raisins.

Fill paper-lined muffin tins full, and bake approximately 20 minutes.

Makes 12 muffins.

Sugar Mill Muffins

The old sugar mill stands where 4th Street runs into Main. Oh golly, I still mind those wonderful muffins they used to serve up over there, with that nutty coconut givin' them a distinctive flavor. You know, folks would come for miles for these, and they'd always come back for more . . . and more.

2 cups flour
1 tablespoon bakin' powder
1/2 teaspoon salt
2/3 cup sugar

1 egg, beaten
1/3 cup oil
1/2 cup milk
1/2 cup sour cream

1 teaspoon coconut extract
1 cup toasted coconut

Preheat your oven to 400°.

Sift the flour with the next 3 ingredients.

Stir in your egg, oil, milk and sour cream, jest till moistened.

Fold in the coconut extract and the coconut.

Fill paper-lined muffin tins full, and bake approximately 20 minutes.

Makes 12 muffins.

Daddy's Special Bran Muffins

Some things stand out clearly in my mind, from those days when I was a young 'un. Jest like those muffins we used to get up at the corner of 2nd Line. Oh, they were beautiful muffins, chock full of all your tastiest fixins'. But I'm tellin' you, this secret recipe of Daddy's comes darn near close to them. With all that maple syrup, molasses and dates they've got tucked into them — why they're jest marvellous.

1 1/2 cups 100% bran cereal
1 1/2 cups milk

1/2 cup whole-wheat flour
1/2 cup all-purpose flour
1 tablespoon bakin' powder
1/2 teaspoon salt

1/3 cup maple syrup
1/3 cup molasses
1 egg, beaten
1/3 cup oil

1 cup chopped, pitted dates

Soak your cereal in the milk for 15 minutes.

Preheat your oven to 400°.

Sift the next 4 ingredients together.

Stir in the next 4 ingredients and bran, jest till moistened.

Fold in your dates.

Fill paper-lined muffin tins full, and bake approximately 20 minutes.

Makes 12 muffins.

Maple Walnut Muffins

Apparently, that old-timer Vic, who sold his farm to Florrie, owned one of your sugarbushes. He sugared along with her the first year, and taught her the ropes. Matter of fact, this recipe is her specialty, a treat she invented after her move up to those parts back in '42.

>   2 **cups flour**
>   1 **tablespoon bakin' powder**
> 1/2 **teaspoon salt**
> 1/4 **cup sugar**
>
>   1 **egg, beaten**
>   1 **cup milk**
> 1/3 **cup butter, melted**
> 1/2 **cup maple syrup**
>   1 **teaspoon maple extract**
>
> 3/4 **cup chopped walnuts**

Preheat your oven to 400°.

Sift flour with the next 3 ingredients.

Add remainin' ingredients except your nuts, and stir jest till moistened.

Fold in your walnuts.

Fill paper-lined muffin tins full, and bake approximately 20 minutes.

Makes 12 muffins.

Rhubarb Streusal Muffins

These muffins are best if you use the young, pink stalks, not the old fellas. And be sure not to eat your roots and leaves.

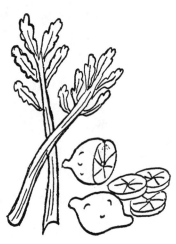

1 1/2 cups chopped rhubarb or 1 package (10 ounces) frozen rhubarb, chopped
1/3 cup water
1 tablespoon lemon juice
1/2 cup sugar
1 1/2 tablespoons cornstarch

2 cups flour
1 tablespoon bakin' powder
1/2 teaspoon salt
1/2 cup sugar

1 egg, beaten
1 cup buttermilk
1/3 cup shortenin', melted

Streusal Topping:
1/2 cup sugar
1/3 cup flour
1/4 cup butter

In a saucepan, combine your first 5 ingredients, and cook over low heat, stirrin' constantly, till thickened. Set aside a spell.

Preheat your oven to 400°.

Sift together the next 4 ingredients.

Stir in egg, buttermilk and shortenin', jest till blended.

Mix the sugar, flour and butter till crumbly.

Fill paper-lined muffin tins 1/2 full, dot with rhubarb fillin', then remainin' batter. Sprinkle crumbly toppin' over. Bake approximately 20 minutes.

Makes 12 muffins.

Oatmeal Buttermilk Muffins

I guess you've all heard about the reputation of our Southern belles, and their buttermilk complexions. What do you think it is? You all would say that it's the climate, but Granny said it was buttermilk and she ought to know. So enjoy these homespun favorites, and grow beautiful at the same time.

  2 cups flour
  1 tablespoon bakin' powder
1/2 teaspoon salt
1/4 cup sugar

1/3 cup honey
  1 egg, beaten
1/3 cup butter, melted
  1 cup buttermilk

3/4 cup rolled oats (quick cookin')
3/4 cup raisins

Preheat your oven to 400°.

Sift flour, bakin' powder, salt and sugar together.

Stir in the next 4 ingredients, jest till moistened.

Fold in the oats and raisins.

Fill paper-lined muffin tins, full, and bake approximately 20 minutes.

Makes 12 muffins.

Irish Soda Muffins

Back in '27, we had Irish folks move in down the way. Margaret used to bring us over her Irish Soda bread regularly, and she'd often invite Granny in to show her how to fix the goodie up. Granny thought it wasn't a bit out of her way to come up with these Irish Soda Muffins, which taste jest like that Old World specialty.

2	cups flour
1 1/2	teaspoons bakin' powder
1 1/2	teaspoons bakin' soda
1/2	teaspoon salt
1	teaspoon caraway seed
1/2	cup sugar
1	egg, beaten
1/3	cup shortenin', melted
1	cup buttermilk
1/2	cup raisins

Preheat your oven to 400°.

Mix together the first 6 ingredients.

Stir in the egg, shortenin' and buttermilk, jest till moistened.

Fold in your raisins.

Fill paper-lined muffin tins full, and bake approximately 20 minutes.

Makes 12 muffins.

Hot Cross Muffins

The next time Good Friday comes around, why not treat your folks to these muffins, 'stead of your regular hot cross buns. Now goin' back to my Granny's day, they say that the MacDonalds up at the farm used to celebrate Easter Sunday by invitin' all the folks for an Easter brunch. Oh, it was supposed to have been a marvellous affair, with sugar-cured ham, and plenty of sweet breads, such as these fruity muffins.

- 2 **cups flour**
- 1 **tablespoon bakin' powder**
- 1/2 **teaspoon salt**
- 1 **teaspoon cinnamon**
- 1/4 **teaspoon nutmeg**
- 1/2 **cup sugar**

- 1 **egg, beaten**
- 1/3 **cup butter, melted**
- 1 **cup milk**

- 3/4 **cup mixed cut, candied fruits**
- 1/2 **cup currants, dried**

- 1 **cup sifted powdered sugar**
- 2 **tablespoons milk**
- 1 **tablespoon butter, melted**
- 1/2 **teaspoon vanilla extract**

Preheat your oven to 400°.

Sift the first 6 ingredients together.

Stir in your egg, butter and milk, jest till blended.

Fold in the fruits.

Fill paper-lined muffin tins full, and bake approximately 20 minutes.

Beat the powdered sugar, milk, butter and vanilla till smooth. Chill.

After the muffins are cooled, pipe a cross with your icing, over each muffin.

Makes 12 muffins.

Peanut Butter Cup Muffins

I mind it was every Tuesday mornin' that Granny used to make her peanut butter cup muffins. Bob, my cousin, who was only a little gadger then, would come runnin' through the cross streets faster than your chicken who got out of the pen. These muffins are marvellous, with a rich chocolate flavor, made extra good with luscious peanut butter chips.

    2 cups flour
    1 tablespoon bakin' powder
1/2 teaspoon salt
    1 cup sugar
1/3 cup cocoa powder

    1 egg, beaten
1/3 cup butter, melted
    1 cup milk

    1 cup Reese's peanut butter chips

Preheat your oven to 400°.

Sift the first 5 ingredients together.

Stir in the egg, butter and milk, jest till blended.

Fold in your peanut butter chips.

Fill paper-lined muffin tins, full, and bake approximately 20 minutes.

Makes 12 muffins.

Surprise Muffins

These muffins became popular in Cat Mash when Granny paid a surprise visit there. It was in the Spring when the housecleanin' was on. But this one time they'd worked so hard that they were all done in by the time Granny arrived. Well, they didn't feel too much like entertainin', so they let Granny take over the bakin', and had a fine time chattin' over these Surprise Muffins and a cup of coffee.

> 2 **cups flour**
> 1 **tablespoon bakin' powder**
> 1/2 **teaspoon salt**
> 1/2 **cup sugar**
>
> 1 **egg, beaten**
> 1/3 **cup shortenin', melted**
> 1/2 **cup milk**
> 1/2 **cup sour cream**
>
> 12 **tablespoons strawberry jelly**

Preheat your oven to 400°.

Sift the first 4 ingredients together.

Stir in the egg, shortenin', milk and sour cream, jest till moistened.

Fill paper-lined muffin tins 1/2 full, place 1 tablespoon of jelly over each muffin, then fill with remainin' batter. Bake approximately 20 minutes.

Makes 12 muffins.

Molasses Muffins

Here's a real old heirloom recipe from my Daddy's side. Now when I say old, I don't mean my Granny's recipe. You have to go way back behind your behind of that. This goes back some 6 generations, and was popular for a spring tonic.

  2 cups flour
  1 tablespoon bakin' powder
1/2 teaspoon salt
1/4 teaspoon ginger
1/2 teaspoon cinnamon
1/4 teaspoon cloves

  1 egg, beaten
1/3 cup butter, melted
1/3 cup table cream

1/3 cup boilin' water
1/3 cup molasses

  1 cup chopped walnuts
1/2 cup raisins

Preheat your oven to 400°.

Sift the first 6 ingredients together.

Stir in the egg, butter and cream, jest till moistened

Dissolve your molasses in the boilin' water. Fold this into your batter.

Fold in the walnuts and raisins.

Fill paper-lined muffin tins full, and bake approximately 20 minutes.

Makes 12 muffins.

Maple Buckwheat Muffins

I mind when I was 17, and worked up at the big plantation house at the end of town. Seem's I'd come into an inheritance of some sort, and had a chance to go over to Europe for a spell. Turns out I had myself a real wing ding, but as the sayin' goes, "There's no place like your home." Mind you, we've had our ups and downs of sickness and hard times, but all told, it's been a wonderful life. I still remember bein' treated to these Maple Buckwheat Muffins on my return to Prospect Junction, on that midnight train.

  1 **cup buckwheat flour**
  1 **cup all-purpose flour**
  1 **tablespoon bakin' powder**
1/2 **teaspoon salt**
1/4 **cup sugar**

  1 **egg, beaten**
1/3 **cup butter, melted**
1/2 **cup milk**
1/2 **cup sour cream**
1/2 **cup maple syrup**
  1 **teaspoon maple extract**

3/4 **cup raisins**

Preheat your oven to 400°.

Sift the first 5 ingredients together.

Stir in the remainin' fixins', except the raisins, jest till moistened.

Fold in the raisins.

Fill paper-lined muffin tins full, and bake approximately 20 minutes.

Makes 12 muffins.

Clover Cream Muffins

Naturally, the bee was the bug in the bonnet, when Granny wanted to collect the honey for these clover cream muffins. Mind you, the mad devil bees, they're not the ones you see today. No sir, them bees has all since disappeared now. You take your average yellowjackets, they're jest upstarts compared to those fellas. So you can imagine that these muffins were a rare treat, usually served up sometime in May.

2 cups flour
1 tablespoon bakin' powder
1/2 teaspoon salt

1 egg, beaten
1/3 cup butter, melted
1 cup light cream
1/2 cup liquid honey

1 cup chopped dates

Preheat your oven to 400°.

Sift the flour, bakin' powder and salt together.

Stir in the next 4 fixins', jest till moistened.

Fold in your chopped dates.

Fill paper-lined muffin tins full, and bake approximately 20 minutes

Makes 12 muffins.

Carob Muffins

Well I declare, if I haven't jest come across this recipe for Carob Muffins. Now no point in thinkin' of carob as your new age ingredient, because see, Granny was bakin' up goodies with it, even then. Now I do remember these on one special occasion, and they were heavenly, with a rich flavor all their own, much like your brown sugar and dates put together.

 2 cups flour
 1 tablespoon bakin' powder
1/2 teaspoon salt
2/3 cup brown sugar, packed

 1 egg, beaten
1/3 cup oil
 1 cup milk

1 1/2 cups carob chips
1/2 cup chopped walnuts

Preheat your oven to 400°.

Sift together the first 4 ingredients.

Stir in your egg, oil and milk, jest till moistened.

Fold in the carob chips and walnuts.

Fill paper-lined muffin tins full, and bake approximately 20 minutes.

Makes 12 muffins.

Pineapple Bacon Muffins

Lord knows how Granny got hold of this muffin recipe, which is a specialty in Pincher Creek, that lumbering town, in the far reaches of your Western Canada. Could be, it was given to her by that rascal Gus, who used to come by. Seem's no one ever did know of his roots, but I jest can't think where else Granny picked this up. I imagine they all stoked up their wood stoves regularly, for these Pineapple Bacon Muffins, which are, I daresay, the best cornmeal muffins that you'll ever eat.

   3 **strips bacon**

   1 **cup flour**
   1 **cup cornmeal**
   1 **tablespoon bakin' powder**
3/4 **teaspoon salt**
   3 **tablespoons brown sugar, packed**

   1 **egg, beaten**
1/3 **cup oil**
   1 **cup buttermilk**

1/2 **cup crushed pineapple, drained**

Fry your bacon till crisp. Drain and set aside a spell.

Preheat your oven to 400°.

Sift the flour with the next 4 ingredients.

Stir in the egg, oil and buttermilk, jest till moistened.

Fold in your pineapple.

Fill paper-lined muffin tins full, crumble bacon atop, and bake approximately 20 minutes.

Makes 12 muffins.

Custard Muffins

Ever since Grandpa got rid of the kickin' cow, our milk jest hasn't been the same. Clover was a mean old cuss, if ever there was one, but she sure know how to give good milk. My Granny invented these Custard Muffins one year when the old critter was still around.

1 1/2 **cups milk**
   2 **tablespoons cornstarch**
1/4 **teaspoon salt**
2/3 **cup sugar**
   1 **egg, beaten**
   1 **teaspoon vanilla extract**

   2 **cups flour**
   1 **tablespoon bakin' powder**
1/2 **teaspoon salt**
2/3 **cup sugar**

   1 **egg, beaten**
1/3 **cup butter, melted**
   1 **cup milk**

Combine the first 6 ingredients and cook over low heat, stirrin' constantly, till thick. Cover with waxed paper, then chill custard in the refrigerator.

Preheat your oven to 400°.

Sift together the next 4 ingredients.

Stir in the egg, butter and milk, jest till blended.

Fill paper-lined muffin tins full, and bake approximately 20 minutes.

When cool, split muffins and fill with custard.

Makes 12 muffins.

Honey Bran Muffins

Darn that Isabel Turner, she's jest dropped in complainin' about her side again. A fool imagination's more like it. You know, whenever I have a batch of muffins in the oven, old Isabel isn't far off. Mind you though, she always leaves feelin' much better than when she came in. She claims that it's on accounta' Granny's delicious Honey Bran Muffins, to name one of the many that she loves.

1 1/2 cups 100% bran cereal
1 1/2 cups milk

1/2 cup whole-wheat flour
1/2 cup all-purpose flour
1 tablespoon bakin' powder
1/2 teaspoon salt

2/3 cup liquid honey
1 egg, beaten
1/3 cup butter, melted

Soak your bran in the milk for 15 minutes.

Preheat your oven to 400°.

Sift the next 4 ingredients together.

Stir in the honey, egg, butter and bran, jest till blended.

Fill paper-lined muffin tins full, and bake approximately 20 minutes.

Makes 12 muffins.

Curious Cat Muffins

These muffins are dedicated to old Ginger, Granny's best loved friend among our critters. Now you take your average calico cat, boy, they hear everything. Like our Ginger, one night she must have heard something, when she came up to Granny's bedroom and pulled the sheets clean off the bed. The next thing Granny knew, why, one of your burglars was pokin' his nose round the family silverware cabinet. Well, Granny wasn't havin' no part of that nohow, and she sent that robber scuttlin' down the stairs, with a shake of her hairbrush. Of course, all of our thanks goes to Ginger.

- **2 cups flour**
- **1 tablespoon bakin' powder**
- **1/2 teaspoon salt**
- **2 teaspoons ginger**
- **1 1/2 teaspoons cinnamon**
- **1/2 teaspoon nutmeg**
- **1/2 cup brown sugar, packed**

- **1/2 cup molasses**
- **1 egg, beaten**
- **1/3 cup butter, melted**
- **1 cup milk**

- **3/4 cup raisins**

Preheat your oven to 400°.

Sift the first 7 ingredients together.

Stir in all the remainin' fixins', except the raisins, jest till moistened.

Fold in your raisins.

Fill paper-lined muffin tins full, and bake approximately 20 minutes.

Makes 12 muffins.

Bran Muffins

Now I'll tell you a little incident, see. Down at the local inn, they used to make the best bran muffins around. But I mind one time when Marianne, the innkeeper, got sick. And what were they to do with all those people askin' for her muffins. So Granny took matters into her own hands that night, and delighted all the customers with these old-fashioned treats.

1 1/2   **cups 100% bran cereal**
1 1/2   **cups buttermilk**
   1   **cup flour**
   1   **tablespoon bakin' powder**
1/2   **teaspoon salt**
   1   **teaspoon cinnamon**
1/4   **teaspoon nutmeg**
2/3   **cup brown sugar, packed**
   1   **egg, beaten**
1/3   **cup butter, melted**
1/2   **cup raisins**

Soak your bran in the buttermilk for 15 minutes.

Preheat your oven to 400°.

Sift together the flour with the next 5 ingredients.

Stir in the egg, butter and your bran fixins', jest till moistened.

Fold in the raisins.

Fill paper-lined muffin tins full, and bake approximately 20 minutes.

Makes 12 muffins.

Polynesian Bran Muffins

Now these muffins are often found in Polynesia, in the South Seas. No, I'm sorry, I told one of my fibs there. Anyways, these are nice for the makin' when you have pineapple left over from your Easter ham.

1 1/2 cups 100% bran cereal
1 1/2 cups milk

  1/2 cup whole-wheat flour
  1/2 cup all-purpose flour
    1 tablespoon bakin' powder
  1/2 teaspoon salt
  2/3 cup brown sugar, packed

    1 egg, beaten
  1/3 cup butter, melted

1 1/2 cups drained, crushed pineapple
  1/4 cup coconut flakes

Soak the bran in the milk for 15 minutes.

Preheat your oven to 400°.

Sift the 5 ingredients followin' together.

Stir in your egg, butter and bran fixins' jest till moistened.

Fold in the pineapple and coconut.

Fill paper-lined muffin tins full, and bake approximately 20 minutes.

Makes 12 muffins.

Chocolate Banana Muffins

Do you mind your chocolate bananas in the ice cream parlor? Round about the time these were invented, Granny decided to try out these muffins, with sensational results. Of course, your local drugstore was the place to go when you wanted to cool off in your annual heatwave.

2 cups flour
1 tablespoon bakin' powder
1/2 teaspoon salt
2/3 cup sugar

1 egg, beaten
1/3 cup butter, melted
1 cup milk

1 banana, chopped
1 cup chocolate chips

Preheat your oven to 400°.

Sift the first 4 ingredients together.

Stir in the egg, butter and milk, jest till blended.

Fold in your banana and chocolate chips.

Fill paper-lined muffin tins full, and bake approximately 20 minutes.

Makes 12 muffins.

Celery Seed Muffins

Now Fanny MacKenzie, as well as bein' postmistress of the town, was the mother of fourteen young 'uns. Seein' as celery is supposed to be good for your nerves, accordin' to our book of home remedies, it made sense for Fanny to bake these up often.

- **2 cups flour**
- **1 tablespoon bakin' powder**
- **1 teaspoon salt**
- **1 teaspoon celery seed**
- **2 tablespoons sugar**

- **1 egg, beaten**
- **1/3 cup butter, melted**
- **1 cup milk**

- **1/4 cup poppyseed**

Preheat your oven to 400°.

Sift the first 5 ingredients together.

Stir in the egg, butter and milk, jest till blended.

Fold in your poppyseed.

Fill paper-lined muffin tins full, and bake approximately 20 minutes.

Makes 12 muffins.

Irish Coffee Muffins

Not all your spiky muffins were made up by your West Indians. Over in Ireland, hard by Tipperary, lived this big sailor called Sean Murphy. Besides sailin' the high seas, he courted an Irish colleen, who was a snorter of a cook. Well, Sean figgered a little excitement was in store for Peggy's bakin', the night he invented these muffins.

> 2 cups flour
> 1 tablespoon bakin' powder
> 1/2 teaspoon salt
> 1/2 cup sugar
>
> 1 egg, beaten
> 1/3 cup butter, melted
> 1/2 cup heavy cream, unwhipped
> 1/4 cup Irish whiskey
> 1/4 cup coffee liqueur

Preheat your oven to 400°.

Sift the first 4 ingredients together.

Stir in the remainin' fixins', jest till moistened.

Fill paper-lined muffin tins full, and bake approximately 20 minutes.

Makes 12 muffins.

Poppyseed Muffins

Many folks have tried to imitate my Granny's poppyseed muffins, but nobody else knew the secret, (the sherry!). I heard tell that over in Henny Marshall's tea shop, they started up a muffin something like my Granny's, featurin' poppyseeds. Well I declare, I tried one out, and not a trace of sherry at all. Old Henny thought she'd come up with our family secret, and I wasn't havin' some.

- 2 cups flour
- 1 tablespoon bakin' powder
- 1/2 teaspoon salt
- 2/3 cup sugar

- 1 egg, beaten
- 1/3 cup butter, melted
- 3/4 cup sour cream
- 1/4 cup cream sherry

- 1/4 cup poppyseed

Preheat your oven to 400°.

Sift the first 4 ingredients together.

Stir in the egg, butter, sour cream and sherry, jest till blended.

Fold in your poppyseed.

Fill paper-lined muffin tins full, and bake approximately 20 minutes.

Makes 12 muffins.

Rice Muffins

These Rice Muffins are old-fashioned favorites. Granny would fix them for us when we were on the recovery route from your measles. Anyway, these taste like a good rice pudding, with jest a touch of cinnamon.

    2 cups flour
    1 tablespoon bakin' powder
1/2 teaspoon cinnamon

    1 egg, beaten
1/3 cup butter, melted
    1 cup milk

1/2 cup liquid honey
    1 cup cooked rice
2/3 cup raisins

Preheat your oven to 400°.

Sift the first 4 ingredients together.

Stir in the egg, butter and milk, jest till moistened.

Pour the honey over the rice and raisins, then fold into your batter.

Fill paper-lined muffin tins full, and bake approximately 20 minutes.

Makes 12 muffins.

Mushroom & Onion Muffins

Upriver from Shadow Pond lies the forest where mushrooms grow in our comin' warm season. Grandpa would come back through the early mornin' loaded down with them, so's Granny could bake up his favorite muffins.

>   2 cups flour
>   1 tablespoon bakin' powder
>   3/4 teaspoon salt
>   2 tablespoons sugar
>
>   1 egg, beaten
>   1/3 cup butter, melted
>   1 cup milk
>
> 1 1/2 cups chopped fresh mushrooms
>   1/3 cup green onions, minced

Preheat your oven to 400°.

Sift the first 4 ingredients together.

Stir in the egg, butter and milk, jest till moistened.

Fold in the mushrooms and onions.

Fill paper-lined muffin tins full, and bake approximately 20 minutes.

Makes 12 muffins.

Cherry Cheese Muffins

Granny's cellar was home for a resident frog, who used to croak happily behind the spring left over from when Jud Bentley owned the place. Granny never bothered the critter, she always believed in your creature comforts. The old cellar overflowed with jams and jellies, ready to be tucked into goodies such as these cherry cheese muffins.

2 cups flour
1 tablespoon bakin' powder
1/2 teaspoon salt
1/2 cup sugar

1 egg beaten
1/3 cup butter, melted
1 cup milk

6 tablespoons cherry preserves
6 tablespoons cream cheese, softened

Preheat your oven to 400°.

Sift the first 4 ingredients together.

Stir in the egg, butter and milk, jest till blended.

Fill paper-lined muffin tins 1/2 full.

Place 1/2 tablespoon cherry preserves, then 1/2 tablespoon cream cheese over each muffin. Cover with remainin' batter, and bake approximately 20 minutes.

Makes 12 muffins.

Summer

Now that the days are hot, it's time to put your feet up, and sit back a spell, while the sun ripens all your fruits and veggies.

Before the critters take the best of your crop, it's a good idea to get your pickins' in early. When the time for berries arrives, some of the best muffins of the year are waitin' for you.

One way to have some real, old-fashioned fun is to hold a family style reunion. Last summer we had kin from all over the country. Most of the folk were purty decent, but there was one young upstart by the name of Jimmy Bates. We was out on a picnic, and the young 'uns were down fishin' on the river. We notices Jimmy with a bag looks mighty suspicious like, but we says nothing. And comin' back on the home bus, what do you think this whippersnapper does? He opens the bag, and purty soon we have crawdaddies explorin' all round your city slicker bus.

Later in the dog days, it's best to relax quiet like, and stay outside while your muffins bake up for your afternoon social.

Blueberry Buckle Muffins

That ol' friendly robin woke me up again. Seein' that he figgers the day has begun, might as well be a conformist, and start the oven up early for my Blueberry Buckle Muffins.

2 cups flour
1 tablespoon bakin' powder
1/2 teaspoon salt
1/2 cup sugar

1 egg, beaten
1/2 cup milk
1/2 cup sour cream
1/3 cup butter, melted
2 teaspoons lemon juice
1 teaspoon grated lemon rind
1 1/2 cups fresh blueberries

Toppin'
1/3 cup sugar
1/3 cup flour
1/4 teaspoon salt
1/4 teaspoon cinnamon
3 tablespoons butter

Preheat your oven to 400°.

Sift the first 4 ingredients,

Stir in the next 6 ingredients jest till moistened.

Fold in your blueberries.

Mix the last set of fixins' till crumbly.

Fill paper-lined muffin tins full with your batter. Sprinkle toppin' over, and bake approximately 20 minutes.

Makes 12 muffins.

Raspberry Muffins

These are one of my Auntie Gladys' specialties. Now Auntie Gladys, she lived way out yonder in your Midwestern areas. I can still taste her raspberry muffins, that literally melt in your mouth. And you know, that would be the longest trip our kin has ever taken out of Toadvine.

      2 cups flour
      1 tablespoon bakin' powder
    1/2 teaspoon salt
    2/3 cup sugar

      1 egg, beaten
    1/3 cup sweet butter, melted
    1/2 cup milk
    1/2 cup sour cream
      1 teaspoon vanilla extract
  1 1/2 cups raspberries, fresh picked

Preheat your oven to 400°.

Sift together your first 4 ingredients.

Stir in the egg, butter, milk, sour cream and vanilla, jest till moistened.

Gently fold in your raspberries.

Fill paper-lined muffin tins full, and bake approximately 20 minutes.

Makes 12 muffins.

Peanut Butter and Jelly Muffins

Now here's Granny's chip off the old block. These rich, velvety muffins are the image of their big mama, those Peanut Butter Muffins. But they like to be a little independent, so they make use of sour cream. But their most winning characteristic is that delectable center of strawberry jelly. All told, the sweetest way to say "I love you" to all the young 'uns in your life.

> 2 **cups flour**
> 1 **tablespoon bakin' powder**
> 3/4 **teaspoon salt**
> 1/2 **cup sugar**
>
> 1 **egg, beaten**
> 1/2 **cup milk**
> 1/2 **cup sour cream**
> 1 **teaspoon vanilla extract**
> 1/4 **cup oil**
> 1/4 **cup crunchy peanut butter**
> 12 **tablespoons strawberry jelly**

Preheat your oven to 400°.

Sift together the first 4 ingredients.

Add the remainin' fixins', except the jelly, and stir jest till moistened.

Fill paper-lined muffin tins 1/2 full, cover with the jelly, (1 tablespoon per muffin), then cover with remainin' batter. Bake for approximately 20 minutes.

Makes 12 muffins.

Strawberry Muffins

I don't know who taught Aunt Bessie from up the Chatahoochee how to bake, but she sure know her onions when it came to makin' these Strawberry Muffins. It doesn't make no never mind whether you use strawberries or boysenberries in these, jest so long as the fruit is fresh.

- 1 1/2 **cups chopped strawberries**
- 3 **tablespoons sugar**
- 3/4 **teaspoon cinnamon**

- 2 **cups flour**
- 1 **tablespoon bakin' powder**
- 1/2 **teaspoon salt**

- 1 **egg, beaten**
- 1/2 **cup milk**
- 1/2 **cup sour cream**
- 1/3 **cup butter, melted**
- 1/2 **cup brown sugar, packed**

Preheat your oven to 400°.

Toss the strawberries with the sugar and cinnamon.

Sift together the next 3 ingredients.

Add remainin' ingredients, stirrin' jest till moistened.

Fold in the strawberries.

Fill paper-lined muffin tins full, and bake approximately 20 minutes.

Makes 12 muffins.

43

Tropical Fruit Muffins

Old Grandpa Bear has slept away most all of the long winter, and now that he's jest wakin' up, he can't think of anything but his blamed stomach. Best to keep these tropical delights off the windowsill till he's finished makin' up for his fast.

2 cups flour
1 tablespoon bakin' powder
1/2 teaspoon salt
1/2 cup sugar

1 egg, beaten
1/3 cup butter, melted
1/2 cup milk
1/2 cup sour cream

1/2 cup coconut, shredded
1/2 cup pineapple, coarsely chopped
1/4 cup maraschino cherries, cut up
1/4 cup macadamia nuts, chopped
1/2 cup dates, chopped

Preheat your oven to 400°.

Sift together the first 4 ingredients.

Stir in your egg, butter, milk and sour cream, jest till blended.

Fold in your remainin' fixins'.

Fill paper-lined muffin tins full, and bake approximately 20 minutes.

Makes 12 muffins.

Sour Cream Pecan Muffins

Every summer, our visitin' tourists head back for home with a bounty of fresh pecans. Many's the farmer who made a regular fortune growin' these nuts in our hot season. At this time of year, it wasn't a bit out of Granny's way to put them into her luscious Sour Cream Pecan Muffins. I must give a word of warning to all you folks on diets, you can never stop with jest one.

> 1 cup finely chopped pecans
> 1/4 cup butter, melted
> 1/4 cup sugar
> 1/3 cup brown sugar, packed
> 1 teaspoon cinnamon
>
> 2 cups flour
> 1 tablespoon bakin' powder
> 1/2 teaspoon salt
> 2/3 cup sugar
>
> 1 egg, beaten
> 1 cup sour cream
> 1/3 cup butter, melted

Mix your first 5 ingredients together and set aside.

Preheat your oven to 400°.

Sift the next 4 ingredients together.

Stir in the egg, sour cream and butter, jest till moistened.

Fill paper-lined muffin tins 1/2 full, cover with 1/2 of your pecan fixins', then fill with remainin' batter, and top with remainin' pecan mixture. Bake approximately 20 minutes.

Makes 12 muffins.

Stone Grist Mill Oatmeal Muffins

When my Mama was a girl, your bathing costumes went clean down to the ankles, I've been told. Must have made it harder for swimmin' down at the old hole by the Stone Grist Mill. Naturally, the oats in these muffins would be crushed right at the mill.

   1 cup whole-wheat flour
   1 cup all-purpose flour
   1 tablespoon bakin' powder
1/2 teaspoon salt
2/3 cup brown sugar, packed

   1 egg, beaten
1/3 cup oil
   1 cup milk

3/4 cup quick-cookin' oats
3/4 cup raisins

Preheat your oven to 400°.

Sift the first 5 ingredients together.

Stir in the egg, oil and milk, jest till moistened.

Fold in the oats and raisins.

Fill paper-lined muffin tins full, and bake approximately 20 minutes.

Makes 12 muffins.

Strawberry Bran Muffins

Here's a recipe from my high falutin' neighbor, who picked it up in your perfumed capital of the world - Paris. Says Michelle - "I didn't always live like this. I used to be jest another resident of Toadvine. Life was insufferably dull, dahling. Then I discovered Paris, with more gourmet vittles than you can shake a stick at. Things like these special Strawberry Bran Muffins. In fact, there probably isn't a thing a girl couldn't get in Paris. Well almost, dahling."

1 1/2 cups 100% bran cereal
1 1/2 cups milk
1/2 cup whole-wheat flour
1/2 cup all-purpose flour
1 tablespoon bakin' powder
1/2 teaspoon salt
2/3 cup brown sugar, packed
1 egg, beaten
1/3 cup butter, melted
1 cup finely chopped strawberries
12 large whole strawberries, stemmed

Soak your bran in the milk for 15 minutes.

Preheat your oven to 400°.

Sift the next 5 ingredients together.

Stir in the egg and butter, jest till blended.

Fold in the finely chopped strawberries.

Fill paper-lined muffin tins full, place a whole strawberry on each muffin, and bake approximately 20 minutes.

Makes 12 muffins.

Key Lime Muffins

These muffins are supposed to originate way down upon the Swanee River. That's where the old folks stay who have plenty of your retirin' money. If you don't live in Floridy, late summer is the best time to pick up fresh limes at your local supermarket.

- 2 **cups flour**
- 1 **tablespoon bakin' powder**
- 1/2 **teaspoon salt**
- 2/3 **cup sugar**

- 1 **egg, beaten**
- 1/3 **cup butter, melted**
- 3/4 **cup milk**
- 1/4 **cup lime juice**
- 2 **tablespoons grated lime peel**

Preheat your oven to 400°.

Sift the first 4 ingredients together.

Stir in the egg, butter, milk, lime juice and peel, jest till moistened.

Fill paper-lined muffin tins full, and bake approximately 20 minutes.

Makes 12 muffins.

Peach Melba Muffins

Toadvine got kinda' quiet after Sam left. To liven things up again, Granny threw one of her famous socials, featurin' these peach melba muffins. I daresay it was the biggest evenin' Granny ever had. Naturally, old Ma Weaver was pokin' her nose around, tryin' to spoil all the fun with a few of her discouragin' words. But a glass of vodka put her in good spirits, and she soon trundled off home, with the recipe for Granny's peach melba muffins tucked safely under her arm.

      2 **cups flour**
      1 **tablespoon bakin' powder**
    1/2 **teaspoon salt**
    1/2 **cup sugar**

      1 **egg, beaten**
    1/3 **cup butter, melted**
      1 **cup milk**

    3/4 **cup peaches, chopped**
    3/4 **cup raspberries**

    1/2 **cup sugar**
    1/3 **cup flour**
    1/4 **cup butter**

Preheat your oven to 400°.

Sift the first 4 ingredients together.

Stir in the egg, butter and milk, jest till moistened.

Fill paper-lined muffin tins 1/2 full.

Cover with fruit, then the remainin' batter.

Mix the sugar, flour and butter together till crumbly.

Sprinkle over your muffins, and bake approximately 20 minutes.

Makes 12 muffins.

Blackcurrant Muffins

Out in the sticks, hard by Pony Hollow, Josey claims to have seen one of your UFO's. I remember that at the time, there was a regular rash of sightins' in the area, seem's like everybody suddenly got your extra-terrestrial fever. Can't say that I've seen anything myself, but I do know the best blackcurrants around make their home here.

        2 cups flour
        1 tablespoon bakin' powder
    1/2 teaspoon salt
        1 cup sugar

        1 egg, beaten
    1/3 cup butter, melted
    1/2 cup sour cream
    1/2 cup milk

        2 teaspoons grated lemon peel
    1 1/2 cups blackcurrants

Preheat your oven to 400°.

Sift the first 4 ingredients together.

Stir in the egg, butter, sour cream and milk, jest till blended.

Fold in your lemon peel and blackcurrants.

Fill paper-lined muffin tins full, and bake approximately 20 minutes.

Makes 12 muffins.

Papaya Muffins

Do you mind that mean old admiral, Captain Bligh? He was connected with quite a mutiny back in 1789. Anyways, that would be about the time that papayas became popular in our New World countries. Also known as the paw paw, they have a flavor much like your melon.

    2 cups flour
    1 tablespoon bakin' powder
1/2 teaspoon salt
2/3 cup sugar

    1 egg, beaten
1/3 cup butter, melted
1/2 cup sour cream
1/2 cup milk
1 1/2 cups papaya, finely chopped

Preheat your oven to 400°.

Sift the first 4 ingredients together.

Stir in the egg, butter, sour cream and milk, jest till moistened.

Fold in your papaya.

Fill paper-lined muffin tins full, and bake approximately 20 minutes.

Makes 12 muffins.

Nectarine Muffins

It's more than likely that you'll detect a hint of your fuzzy friend, the peach, in these muffins. In fact, they're related to that fruit, makin' it a family affair. There's some that hold, and your encyclopedias too, that the nectarine tree sometimes gives out peaches. And my gol, if your peach tree doesn't do the same with it's kissin' cousin. These 'Nuts of Persia' make for excellent muffins.

        2 **cups flour**
        1 **tablespoon bakin' powder**
    1/2 **teaspoon salt**
    1/2 **cup sugar**

        1 **egg, beaten**
    1/3 **cup butter, melted**
    1/2 **cup sour cream**
    1/2 **cup milk**
    1 1/2 **cups nectarines, peeled and chopped**

Preheat your oven to 400°.

Sift the first 4 ingredients together.

Stir in the egg, butter, sour cream and milk, jest till blended.

Fold in your nectarines.

Fill paper-lined muffin tins full, and bake approximately 20 minutes.

Makes 12 muffins.

Bing Cherry Muffins

This recipe was given to us by our Great-Aunt, who lived in Cherry Valley way up yonder in your state of New York. Great-Aunt Dianne says she searches her orchard to find the finest, plumpest cherries for these delightful muffins. Dianne's house is so big that she can put up as many as fifteen kin for the night.

2	cups flour
1	tablespoon bakin' powder
1/2	teaspoon salt
2/3	cup sugar
1	egg, beaten
1/3	cup butter, melted
1/2	cup sour cream
1/2	cup milk
2	teaspoons grated lemon peel
1 1/2	cups Bing cherries, pitted and halved (fresh or frozen)

Preheat your oven to 400°.

Sift together the first 4 ingredients.

Stir in your egg, butter, sour cream and milk, jest till moistened.

Fold in the peel and cherries.

Fill paper-lined muffin tins full, and bake approximately 20 minutes.

Makes 12 muffins.

Juicy Peach Muffins

When our Cory failed to return for supper one evening, a search party was sent to find him. Turns out he was explorin' the DeSoto Caverns hard by, and plumb lost his way. We all celebrated his return with a plateful of Granny's Juicy Peach Muffins.

2	**cups flour**
1	**tablespoon bakin' powder**
1/2	**teaspoon salt**
1/2	**cup sugar**
1	**egg, beaten**
1/2	**cup milk**
1/2	**cup sour cream**
1/3	**cup butter, melted**
1	**teaspoon vanilla extract**
1 1/2	**cups chopped peaches, peeled and stoned**

Preheat your oven to 400°.

Sift together your first 4 ingredients.

Mix in the egg, milk, sour cream, butter and vanilla, jest till moistened.

Fold in your peaches.

Fill paper-lined muffin tins full, and bake approximately 20 minutes.

Makes 12 muffins.

Gooseberry Muffins

These tart little guys are often thought of as something to get around, like your Saturday morning housework. One taste of these delicious Gooseberry Muffins should have folks changin' their minds.

      2 **cups flour**
      1 **tablespoon bakin' powder**
  1/2 **teaspoon salt**
  1/2 **cup sugar**

      1 **egg, beaten**
  1/3 **cup butter, melted**
      1 **cup buttermilk**

1 1/2 **cups gooseberries (fresh)**

Preheat your oven to 400°.

Sift the first 4 ingredients together.

Stir in the egg, butter and buttermilk, jest till moistened.

Fold in your gooseberries.

Fill paper-lined muffin tins full, and bake approximately 20 minutes.

Makes 12 muffins.

Watercress Muffins

Mind you, when the temperature's soarin' and your spirits are laggin' seem's to make sense to forget dinner and have an afternoon social. Try these Watercress Muffins, served with some slices of cold Virginny style ham.

- **2 cups flour**
- **1 tablespoon bakin' powder**
- **3/4 teaspoon salt**
- **dash dry mustard**
- **2 tablespoons sugar**

- **1 egg, beaten**
- **1 cup milk**
- **1/3 cup butter, melted**

- **1/2 cup finely chopped watercress**
- **2 tablespoons minced green onion**

Preheat your oven to 400°.

Sift the flour with the next 4 ingredients.

Stir in the egg, milk and butter, jest till moistened.

Fold in your watercress and green onion.

Fill paper-lined muffin tins full, and bake approximately 20 minutes.

Makes 12 muffins.

Redcurrant Muffins

It's nice to gather the currants for these ruby studded muffins in the cool of the evening, when the heat of the day has worn off. I'll never forget the year they opened the Hearth Oven Bakery down the way. Well listen, when that opened, they used to make up a Redcurrant Muffin that was the pride of Toadvine. Somehow, Granny wangled the recipe from the owners, and here it is for you all now.

1 1/2 **cups stemmed redcurrants**
   2 **tablespoons sugar**
   2 **tablespoons flour**

   2 **cups flour**
   1 **tablespoon bakin' powder**
1/2 **teaspoon salt**
2/3 **cup sugar**

   1 **egg, beaten**
1/3 **cup sweet butter, melted**
   1 **cup buttermilk**

Preheat your oven to 400°.

Toss the redcurrants with the next 2 ingredients.

Sift flour, bakin' powder, salt and sugar together.

Stir in the egg, butter and buttermilk, jest till blended.

Gently fold in your redcurrants.

Fill paper-lined muffin tins full, and bake approximately 20 minutes.

Makes 12 muffins.

Pineapple Muffins

Old Ma Weaver, who is jest comin' down the road, looks a funny sight. Yes sir, she certainly is a funny sight, with her muffins tucked up in her apron, headin' toward town. And do you know what she is going to do there? She is going to try sellin' her muffins to the local bakery. Well I declare, if she doesn't stop at nothing to make her muffins more popular than Granny's. At this moment, I have some Pineapple Muffins bakin' up, that are sure to put Ma Weaver's to shame.

      2 **cups flour**
      1 **tablespoon bakin' powder**
  1/2 **teaspoon salt**
  1/2 **cup sugar**

      1 **egg, beaten**
  1/3 **cup butter, melted**
      1 **cup milk**
  1 1/2 **cups pineapple chunks, drained**

      2 **tablespoons sugar**
  1/2 **teaspoon cinnamon**

Preheat your oven to 400°.

Sift the first 4 ingredients together.

Stir in your egg, butter and milk, jest till blended.

Fill paper-lined muffin tins half full, place pineapple chunks over, then fill with remainin' batter.

Combine your last 2 ingredients, and sprinkle atop the muffins. Bake approximately 20 minutes.

Makes 12 muffins.

Chocolate Chip Muffins

These muffins will be feudin' with your chocolate chip cookies for first place in popularity. You probably wouldn't remember when they first opened up that Toll House back in your 1920's. No, maybe you can remember. Anyway, they made the best chocolate chip cookies in America in the old days.

2 cups flour
1 tablespoon bakin' powder
1/2 teaspoon salt
1/3 cup sugar
1/3 cup brown sugar

1 egg, beaten
1/3 cup sweet butter, melted
1/2 cup milk
1/2 cup sour cream

1 1/2 cups chocolate chips
1 cup chopped walnuts

Preheat your oven to 400°.

Sift the first 4 ingredients together.

Stir in the egg, butter, milk and sour cream, jest till blended.

Fold in 1 cup of your chocolate chips and the walnuts.

Fill paper-lined muffin tins full, sprinkle with the remainin' chocolate chips, and bake approximately 20 minutes.

Makes 12 muffins.

Blackberry Muffins

Those pesky little thorns you're feelin' in your side while pickin' these berries are well worth it when you bite into one of these steamin' hot muffins, burstin' with fruit. So battle your thorns under all them trailers, so's you can get the best pickins' for these special treats.

- 2 cups flour
- 1 tablespoon bakin' powder
- 1/2 teaspoon salt
- 1 cup sugar

- 1 egg, beaten
- 1/3 cup sweet butter, melted
- 1/2 cup milk
- 1/2 cup sour cream

- 1 1/2 cups fresh blackberries
- 1/2 cup chopped pecans

Preheat your oven to 400°.

Sift the first 4 ingredients, jest till moistened.

Fold in the blackberries and pecans.

Fill paper-lined muffin tins full, and bake approximately 20 minutes.

Makes 12 muffins.

Tomato Muffins

When the harvest moon climbed high up in the eastern sky, we knew that summer was wanin'. And what better way to end those lazy days, than to go up the country to my Cousin Nell's, where we all enjoyed eatin' her Tomato Muffins.

> 1 cup flour
> 1 cup wholewheat flour
> 1 tablespoon bakin' powder
> 3/4 teaspoon salt
> 1/2 teaspoon oregano
> 2 tablespoons sugar
> 1/4 cup grated Parmesan cheese
>
> 1 egg, beaten
> 1 cup buttermilk
> 1/3 cup butter, melted
>
> 1 fresh tomato, peeled, seeded and coarsely chopped

Preheat your oven to 400°.

Sift the first 7 ingredients together.

Stir in the egg, buttermilk and butter, jest till blended.

Fold in your tomato.

Fill paper-lined muffin tins full, and bake approximately 20 minutes.

Makes 12 muffins.

Peach Bran Muffins

I'll never forget Great-Aunt Lizzie's Peach Bran Muffins. Now at that time, Lizzie was ninety years old if she was a day, bein' Granny's older sister. But jest goes to show you how your bakin' know-how runs in the family.

1 1/2 cups 100% bran cereal
1 1/2 cups milk
1/2 cup whole-wheat flour
1/2 cup all-purpose flour
1 tablespoon bakin' powder
1/2 teaspoon salt
1/2 teaspoon cinnamon
2/3 cup brown sugar, packed
1 egg, beaten
1/3 cup butter, melted
1 1/2 cups finely chopped peaches, peeled and stoned

Soak the bran in the milk for 15 minutes.

Preheat your oven to 400°.

Sift together your next 6 fixins'.

Stir in the egg and butter, jest till moistened.

Fold in your peaches.

Fill paper-lined muffin tins full, and bake approximately 20 minutes.

Makes 12 muffins.

Kiwi Muffins

Most folks may find recipes for Australia's kiwi fruit hard to find. Well, it depends on the circumstances. You will find the fancy green specialty a very delicious thing, when it is done up in these muffins.

        2 cups flour
        1 tablespoon bakin' powder
    1/2 teaspoon salt
    2/3 cup sugar

        1 egg, beaten
    1/3 cup butter, melted
        1 cup milk

        1 tablespoon grated lemon rind
    1 1/2 cups peeled kiwis, chopped
        3/4 cup walnuts, chopped

Preheat your oven to 400°.

Sift the first 4 ingredients together.

Stir in the egg, butter and milk, jest till blended.

Fold in your lemon rind, kiwis and nuts.

Fill paper-lined muffin tins full, and bake approximately 20 minutes.

Makes 12 muffins.

Cherry Nut Muffins

In the old days, cherry pickin' time gave folks a chance to savor some of the best pies and cakes of the year. Not to mention your annual home cannin'. Oh my word, Granny used to can 150 jars of the stuff. Well, you'd be surprised how fast it went, what with all the kin 'round so often. Of course, when you get to this age, you don't can like you used to. I wanted to do up some cherry jam this summer, but that darned rainy spell gave me a bad case of your rheumatism. So I settled instead, for these tasty muffins.

- 2 **cups flour**
- 1 **tablespoon bakin' powder**
- 1/2 **teaspoon salt**
- 2/3 **cup sugar**

- 1 **egg, beaten**
- 1/3 **cup butter, melted**
- 1 **cup milk**

- 3/4 **cup chopped pecans**
- 3/4 **cup chopped maraschino cherries**

Preheat your oven to 400°.

Sift the first 4 ingredients together.

Stir in the egg, butter and milk, jest till blended.

Fold in your pecans and cherries.

Fill paper-lined muffin tins full, and bake approximately 20 minutes.

Makes 12 muffins.

Blue Heaven Muffins

This recipe is from one of Granny's friends, who lived hard by Glasgow, Scotland. If there's one thing them Scots know how to cook up, it's your oatmeal. Of course, oats became popular in your average teatime treats, such as scones and biscuits. Harry Ferguson claims that this muffin recipe was handed down from his great-aunt, who baked them up in her little brick oven.

1 3/4 cups flour
1 tablespoon bakin' powder
1/2 teaspoon salt
2/3 cup sugar

1 egg, beaten
1/3 cup butter, melted
1 cup milk

3/4 cup rolled oats
1 1/2 cups blueberries

Preheat your oven to 400°.

Sift the first 4 ingredients together.

Stir in the egg, butter and milk, jest till blended.

Fold in your oats and blueberries.

Fill paper-lined muffin tins full, and bake approximately 20 minutes.

Makes 12 muffins.

Pistachio Muffins

The well went dry the first of July, so's we had to get the darned thing cleaned out, and then lug water from a spring hard by. With all that extry work, we were hungry as bears, so's you won't be surprised to hear that ten of these muffins disappeared in one night.

2 cups flour
1 tablespoon bakin' powder
1/2 teaspoon salt
2/3 cup sugar

1 egg, beaten
1/3 cup oil
1 cup milk

1 teaspoon pistachio extract
1 cup chopped pistachios
few drops green food coloring (optional)

Preheat your oven to 400°.

Sift the first 4 ingredients together.

Stir in the egg, oil and milk, jest till blended.

Fold in your remainin' fixins'.

Fill paper-lined muffin tins full, and bake approximately 20 minutes.

Makes 12 muffins

Chimney Bay Muffins

Any of your tart berries will be fine in these muffins, but Granny always made use of the elderberries that ran wild along the shores of Chimney Bay. Now these here elderberries, along with your raspberries and brambleberries, are the flavors that made Chimney Bay famous. One of your most delectable wild places around these parts, it attracts many outside visitors, who come early in the day to get their pickins' in, so's they can take them home to enjoy with your thick cream and honey. I think you all should find these unusual muffins some of the most mouth-watering you have ever eaten.

　　2　cups flour
　　1　tablespoon bakin' powder
　1/2　teaspoon salt
　　1　cup sugar

　　1　egg, beaten
　1/3　cup butter, melted
　1/2　cup sour cream
　1/2　cup milk

　1　1/2　cups elderberries

Preheat your oven to 400°.

Sift the first 4 ingredients together.

Stir in the egg, butter, sour cream and milk, jest till blended.

Fold in your elderberries.

Fill paper-lined muffin tins full, and bake approximately 20 minutes.

Makes 12 muffins.

Mint Muffins

Before you raise your eyebrows at this muffin combination, I invite you to try one of these with your roast lamb one Sunday. I guarantee you satisfaction. (and then some). And say, that reminds me, Granny got hold of this recipe over at our annual fall fair, hard by Kickin' Cow Pass. So you can be sure you have the makins' for some marvellous muffins here, from your mint patch.

        2 cups flour
        1 tablespoon bakin' powder
    1/2 teaspoon salt
    1/4 cup sugar

        1 egg, beaten
    1/3 cup butter, melted
    3/4 cup milk

    1/4 cup vinegar
        1 cup fresh mint leaves, finely chopped

Preheat your oven to 400°.

Sift the first 4 ingredients together.

Stir in the egg, butter and milk, jest till blended.

Pour the vinegar over your mint leaves, then quickly fold into the batter.

Fill paper-lined muffin tins full, and bake approximately 20 minutes.

Makes 12 muffins.

Canta-Melon Muffins

I mind the heatwave we had back in 1915. At that time, it was Pat O'Connor, your local skinnydipper, who stirred things up the most. He must have been your flasher of the day, dashin' all over the beaches, and even showin' up in town in his birthday suit. That's when the sheriff had him ridden out of town on a rail. One thing the folks did before he left, was to throw a last supper for him. Naturally, Granny pitched in her two cents worth, with these canta-melon muffins.

2	cups flour
1	tablespoon bakin' powder
1/2	teaspoon salt
1/2	cup sugar
1	egg, beaten
1/3	cup butter, melted
1/2	cup sour cream
1/2	cup milk
1 1/2	cups chopped cantaloupe

Preheat your oven to 400°.

Sift the first 4 ingredients together.

Stir in the egg, butter, sour cream and milk, jest till blended.

Fold in your cantaloupe.

Fill paper-lined muffin tins full, and bake approximately 20 minutes.

Makes 12 muffins.

Lingonberry Muffins

The thing that really defeated these muffins in Sweden was the fact that nobody there gave a darn about them. Everybody was up to their ears in lingonberries, and I guess they just wanted a muffin made up of bran and berries. Somehow, the idea for makin' these muffins popped into my Granny's head one day, to the delight of all our kin.

2 cups flour
1 tablespoon bakin' powder
1/2 teaspoon salt
1 cup sugar

1 egg, beaten
1/3 cup butter, melted
1/2 cup sour cream
1/2 cup milk

1 1/2 cups lingonberries
3/4 cup walnuts, chopped

Preheat your oven to 400°.

Sift the first 4 ingredients together.

Stir in the egg, butter, sour cream and milk, jest till moistened.

Fold in your lingonberries and nuts.

Fill paper-lined muffin tins full, and bake approximately 20 minutes.

Makes 12 muffins.

Huckleberry Muffins

If you have the fortune to camp out at Little Dog State Park one fine summer weekend, be sure to take the side road hard by Fiddlehead Creek. Don't let them 'squities stop you from pickin' at least one or two bushels of these wonderful berries. One of the more curious happenins' out at Little Dog was the affair with Ned Hanlan, a forest ranger of the state. He was jest pickin' around one day, mindin' his own business, when all of a sudden he heard a great roar. Well, he went around the bend, hard by Gum Point, and came face to face with a huge critter. They still can't figger out jest what it was, some say it could have been your Bigfoot, who must have been on vacation from Californy. Anyways, seem's like there's more than 'squities to keep you all from enjoyin' these huckleberry muffins.

    2 **cups flour**
    1 **tablespoon bakin' powder**
1/2 **teaspoon salt**
1/2 **cup sugar**

    1 **egg, beaten**
1/3 **cup butter, melted**
1/2 **cup sour cream**
1/2 **cup milk**
1 1/2 **cups huckleberries**

Preheat your oven to 400°.

Sift together the first 4 ingredients.

Stir in your egg, butter, sour cream and milk, jest till moistened.

Fold in your huckleberries.

Fill paper-lined muffin tins full, and bake approximately 20 minutes.

Makes 12 muffins.

Loganberry Muffins

The idea for makin' these muffins popped into Granny's head one day, after Cousin Eileen said she lost the recipe. Just you imagine how she felt at the family social when everyone said "So, Eileen finally gave up the recipe."

2 **cups flour**
1 **tablespoon bakin' powder**
1/2 **teaspoon salt**
1 **cup sugar**

1 **egg, beaten**
1/3 **cup butter, melted**
1 **cup buttermilk**

1 1/2 **cups loganberries**

Preheat your oven to 400°.

Sift the first 4 ingredients together.

Stir in the egg, butter and buttermilk, jest till blended.

Fold in your loganberries.

Fill paper-lined muffin tins full, and bake approximately 20 minutes.

Makes 12 muffins.

Pina Colada Muffins

These muffins were invented by Grandpa one summer when it was too wet to plow. But as soon as the rainy spell passed, he was soon out with his horse, Mr. Humphries, again. You know what they say about two cooks in your kitchen. But my gol, I wonder if it makes sense, whenever I taste one of these coconut rum specialities.

>   2 cups flour
>   1 tablespoon bakin' powder
>   1/2 teaspoon salt
>   1/2 cup sugar
>
>   1 egg, beaten
>   1/3 cup butter, melted
>   1/2 cup coconut rum liqueur
>   1/2 cup pineapple juice
>
>   1/2 cup crushed pineapple, drained
>   1/2 cup coconut, flaked

Preheat your oven to 400°.

Sift the first 4 ingredients together.

Stir in the egg, butter, liqueur and pineapple juice, jest till moistened.

Fold in the pineapple and coconut.

Fill paper-lined muffin tins full, and bake approximately 20 minutes.

Makes 12 muffins.

Mixed Fruit Muffins

Poor old Uncle Bill, he was a good farmer and had a good business head, but he didn't know beans about growin' fruit. So the results, he'd usually come down to Grandpa's orchard for some fruit to tuck into his special muffins. And wait till you try these, plump and juicy, with the wealth of your orchard put up in a muffin.

>   2 **cups flour**
>   1 **tablespoon bakin' powder**
> 1/2 **teaspoon salt**
> 2/3 **cup sugar**
>
>   1 **egg, beaten**
> 1/3 **cup shortenin', melted**
> 1/2 **cup milk**
> 1/2 **cup sour cream**
>
> 1/2 **cup finely chopped peaches, peeled and stoned**
> 1/2 **cup fresh blueberries**
> 1/4 **cup seedless grapes, coarsely chopped**

Preheat your oven to 400°.

Sift together the first 4 ingredients.

Stir in the egg, shortenin', milk and sour cream, jest till moistened.

Fold in your fruits.

Fill paper-lined muffin tins full, and bake approximately 20 minutes.

Makes 12 muffins.

Fall

Here's the season of your mists and mellow fruitfulness, as the poets say.

It's time to gather up all your harvest collectables for the winter, such as apples and onions. These keep a long time stored up in your root cellar.

Round about this time, we all pay our annual visit to the Big C Possum Ranch. This is in the Black Belt region, hard by Tuscaloosa, for any of you folks wishin' to come on down. Anyways, this one year, we found a homeless baby possum whose mama and daddy had up and died, and none other of the critters had any motherin' instinct to spare. Big C Possum Ranch took her in hand, and little Suzy grew up to be a mama possum herself.

After a day in the crisp, nippy air, we came home to the first aroma of Granny's muffins, waftin' out of the oven.

Corn Muffins

These corn muffins are excellent served alongside jambalaya. Seems the Cajuns and the Creoles had been feudin' over their rights to this dish for years. They never did get the matter fixed up, so they figgered they might as well as share the recipe.

1	**cup yellow cornmeal**
1 1/4	**cups buttermilk**
1	**cup flour**
1 1/2	**teaspoons bakin' powder**
1 1/2	**teaspoons bakin' soda**
1	**teaspoon salt**
1/3	**cup sugar**
1	**egg, beaten**
1/4	**cup molasses**
1/3	**cup butter, melted**
1 1/2	**cups frozen corn kernels, defrosted**

Preheat your oven to 400°.

Combine your cornmeal and buttermilk, and set aside for 20 minutes.

Sift the flour, bakin' powder, bakin' soda, salt and sugar together.

Stir in the egg, molasses and butter, along with your cornmeal fixins', jest till moistened.

Fold in your corn kernels.

Fill paper-lined muffin tins full, and bake approximately 20 minutes.

Makes 12 muffins.

Fat Jack Muffins

Back of the bayou lies the home of the mud oysters. I don't rightly know their correct name, but old Jack always called them that. Pair these up with Jack's fat muffins, and you'll have some of the best eatin' you'll ever know.

2 cups flour
1 tablespoon bakin' powder
3/4 teaspoon salt
2 tablespoons sugar

1 egg, beaten
1/3 cup oil
1 cup milk

1 cup shredded cheese
6 slices bacon, fried and crumbled

Preheat your oven to 400°.

Sift the first 4 ingredients together.

Stir in the egg, oil and milk, jest till blended.

Fold in the cheese and bacon.

Fill paper-lined muffin tins full, and bake approximately 20 minutes.

Makes 12 muffins.

Pumpkin Muffins

Now that the old oak tree is turnin' gold, an eerie feelin' is all about. Halloween is creepin' up, and folks are extry careful jest now to steer clear of the turnoff leadin' to old Hattie's shack. Best to stay in safe and snug, and bake up a batch of my Granny's Pumpkin Muffins.

- 2 cups flour
- 1 tablespoon bakin' powder
- 1/2 teaspoon salt
- 1/2 teaspoon ginger
- 1/4 teaspoon nutmeg
- 1 teaspoon cinnamon
- dash cloves, ground
- 2/3 cup sugar

- 1 egg, beaten
- 1 cup sour cream
- 3 tablespoons orange marmalade (not bitter)
- 1/3 cup oil
- 1 cup pumpkin (mashed or tinned)

Preheat your oven to 400°.

Sift the first 8 ingredients together.

Stir in the remainin' ingredients, jest till blended.

Fill paper-lined muffin tins full, and bake approximately 20 minutes.

Makes 12 muffins.

Plantation Muffins

These rich, double cream muffins call to mind those wonderful midnight lunches at my Auntie Gloria's gorgeous mansion. Oh land, that was your house and a half, as they say now. We young 'uns would get ourselves lost in the maze hard by, while the older folk talked on the screened-in porch. And we all were jest waitin' for these luxurious muffins to be served up.

- 2 cups flour
- 1 tablespoon bakin' powder
- 1/2 teaspoon salt
- 2/3 cup sugar

- 1 egg, beaten
- 1/3 cup sweet butter, melted
- 1/2 cup whipping cream, unwhipped
- 1/2 cup half and half
- 1 teaspoon vanilla extract

- 1 small orange, grated
- 3/4 cup chopped walnuts

Preheat your oven to 400°.

Sift together the first 4 ingredients.

Stir in the egg, butter and creams, also your vanilla, jest till blended.

Fold the orange and nuts into the batter.

Fill paper-lined muffin tins full, and bake approximately 20 minutes.

Makes 12 muffins.

Peanut Butter Muffins

Folks down here know peanuts better as goober nuts. These goobers have their roots deep down in the hearts of all the young 'uns when it comes to peanut butter. That should make these muffins popular with the younger set.

> 2 cups flour
> 1 tablespoon bakin' powder
> 3/4 teaspoon salt
> 3/4 cup sugar
>
> 1 egg, beaten
> 1 cup buttermilk
> 1 teaspoon vanilla extract
> 1/4 cup oil
> 1/4 cup peanut butter, smooth
>
> 1 cup chopped peanuts, unsalted

Preheat your oven to 400°.

Sift together the first 4 ingredients.

Add the egg and remainin' ingredients, except the peanuts, jest till moistened.

Fold in your peanuts.

Fill paper-lined muffin tins full, and bake approximately 20 minutes.

Makes 12 muffins.

Apple Cinnamon Muffins

Of all the muffins Granny ever made, these are my favorites. As my brother said one time when we were talkin' about the old days, he believes they are the finest apple muffins ever made. If you don't agree, jest try findin' a better recipe for these moist, delectable treats anywhere across the country.

1 1/2 cups finely chopped apples, peeled and cored
1 teaspoon cinnamon
2 tablespoons brown sugar, packed
3 tablespoons butter, melted

2 cups flour
1 tablespoon bakin' powder
1/2 teaspoon salt
1/2 cup brown sugar, packed
1/4 teaspoon cloves
1 teaspoon cinnamon

1 egg, beaten
1 cup evaporated milk
1/3 cup butter, melted

1/4 cup brown sugar, packed
1 teaspoon cinnamon
1/4 teaspoon ground cloves

Mix your apples with the cinnamon, brown sugar and butter. Cover and steam over low heat for two minutes.

Preheat your oven to 400°.

Sift the next 6 ingredients together.

Stir in the egg, milk and butter, jest till blended.

Fold in your apple fixins'.

Combine the remainin' ingredients till crumbly.

Fill paper-lined muffin tins full with your batter. Sprinkle crumbly toppin' over, and bake approximately 20 minutes.

Makes 12 muffins.

Whole Wheat Muffins

Sometimes it's nice jest to get back to your basics. That's the time to make these home style, natural muffins. This recipe has been handed down from a descendant of Great Granny's, and the muffins are made according to her secret formula.

1 cup flour
1 cup whole wheat flour
1 tablespoon bakin' powder
1/2 teaspoon salt
1/2 cup brown sugar, packed
1 teaspoon cinnamon

1 egg, beaten
1/3 cup oil
1 cup milk

1 cup chopped dates
1/2 cup chopped walnuts

Preheat your oven to 400°.

Sift the first 6 ingredients together.

Stir in the egg, oil and milk, jest till blended.

Fold in your dates and nuts.

Fill paper-lined muffin tins full, and bake approximately 20 minutes.

Makes 12 muffins.

Pear Cheese Muffins

Here's a happy marriage of flavors from your Harvest Home. Granny has paired up Miss Bartlett Pear and Mr. Cheddar Cheese for a long life together. We always did hold that Granny was your greatest matchmaker.

       2 **cups flour**
       1 **tablespoon bakin' powder**
     1/2 **teaspoon salt**
     2/3 **cup sugar**

       1 **egg, beaten**
       1 **cup milk**
     1/3 **cup shortenin', melted**

       1 **cup grated Bartlet pears, peeled and cored**
       1 **cup grated Cheddar cheese**

Preheat your oven to 400°.

Sift the first 4 ingredients together.

Stir in the egg, milk and shortenin', jest till blended.

Fold in your pears and cheese.

Fill paper-lined muffin tins full, and bake approximately 20 minutes.

Makes 12 muffins.

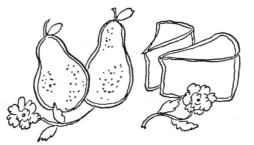

Plum Kuchen Muffins

One year we had folks visitin' from the Black Forest region of Germany. Along with a bit of weight, we all gained a new muffin recipe. Here is your Plum Kuchen of the muffin world.

2 cups flour
1 tablespoon bakin' powder
1/2 teaspoon salt
1/2 cup sugar

1 egg, beaten
1/2 cup milk
1/2 cup sour cream
1/3 cup butter, melted

2 teaspoons grated lemon rind
1 1/2 cups chopped plums, peeled and stoned

1/3 cup sugar
1/3 cup flour
1/4 teaspoon salt
1/4 teaspoon cinnamon
3 tablespoons butter

Preheat your oven to 400°.

Sift the first 4 ingredients together.

Add your egg, milk, sour cream and butter, and stir jest till moistened.

Fold in the lemon rind and plums.

Fill paper-lined muffin tins full, set aside.

Combine remainin' fixins' till crumbly, sprinkle over your muffins, and bake approximately 20 minutes.

Makes 12 muffins.

Ginny's Pear Bran Muffins

I mind a friend of Grandpa's who used to own an acreage over at Port de Lucy. I can't remember his name now, but his wife, Ginny, had the fixins' right at hand for these muffins, because, see, her husband specialized in growin' Bartlett pears. And the results — a juicy treat of a muffin, good enough for your Sunday company.

1 1/2 cups 100% bran cereal
1 1/2 cups milk
1/2 cup whole-wheat flour
1/2 cup all-purpose flour
1 tablespoon bakin' powder
1/2 teaspoon salt
1 teaspoon cinnamon
2/3 cup brown sugar, packed
1 egg, beaten
1/3 cup butter, melted
1 1/2 cups finely chopped Bartlet pears,
    pared and cored

Soak your bran in the milk for 15 minutes.

Preheat your oven to 400°.

Sift together the next 6 ingredients.

Stir in the egg and butter, jest till moistened.

Fold in your pears.

Fill paper-lined muffin tins full, and bake approximately 20 minutes.

Makes 12 muffins.

Whole-Wheat Squash Muffins

When Granny first caught wind of this recipe for whole-wheat squash muffins, why, she didn't quite know what to do with it. We'd all had squash whipped up like your taters, but we'd never had it put up in a muffin before. It took only one bite to convince Granny to call in the neighbors for afternoon tea.

    1 cup whole-wheat flour
    1 cup all-purpose flour
    1 tablespoon bakin' powder
1/2 teaspoon salt
    1 teaspoon cinnamon
1/2 teaspoon ginger
1/4 teaspoon cloves, ground
2/3 cup brown sugar, packed

    1 egg, beaten
1/3 cup oil
    1 cup yogurt
    1 cup mashed squash

Preheat your oven to 400°.

Sift together the first 8 ingredients.

Stir in the remainin' fixins', jest till moistened.

Fill paper-lined muffin tins full, and bake approximately 20 minutes.

Makes 12 muffins.

Apple Date Muffins

Back in the autumn of '25, we had one of the best years on record for apples. Granny figgered it was the perfect opportunity to stage a harvest bake. And you know, the next mornin', she looked out the window, she nearly died. Well, sombody had picked the tree purty near clean. Folks nearby said nothin' was left of the corn crop but the stubbins. Seem's some delivery van had made off with darn near the whole harvest. We never did find the mysterious night raider, but Granny's Apple Date Muffins were doubly appreciated the next year.

- 1 cup whole-wheat flour
- 1 cup all-purpose flour
- 1 tablespoon bakin' powder
- 1/2 teaspoon salt
- 1 teaspoon cinnamon
- 1/2 teaspoon allspice
- 1 cup brown sugar, packed

- 1 tablespoon instant coffee powder
- 1/2 cup boilin' water

- 1 egg, beaten
- 1/3 cup butter, melted
- 1/2 cup milk

- 2 apples, pared, cored and grated
- 1 cup chopped dates
- 1/2 cup chopped walnuts

Preheat your oven to 400°.

Sift the first 7 ingredients together.

Dissolve the coffee in the boilin' water.

Stir this, along with your egg, butter and milk, into the flour mixture, jest till moistened.

Fold in the remainin' fixins'.

Fill paper-lined muffin tins full, and bake approximately 20 minutes.

Makes 12 muffins.

Italian Zuccotto Muffins

I mind the barn fire we had one year, down by Pine Ridge Bend. Well, they got all the critters out safe, but the barn itself was all but gone. They don't rightly know how the whole thing got started, but in those days the chores were usually done by lantern-light. Anyways, the folks all around pitched in with money to help restore the barn, and you know, they got up enough for a new outhouse too, what with everyone helpin' out. We all had a housewarmin' party to celebrate, and that's where I first tried these Italian Zuccotto Muffins, a recipe of Mrs. Orsini's.

    2 **cups flour**
    1 **tablespoon bakin' powder**
1/2 **teaspoon salt**
    1 **cup sugar**

    1 **egg, beaten**
1/3 **cup butter, melted**
1/2 **cup half-and-half**
1/4 **cup muscatel wine**
1/4 **cup brandy**

    1 **cup blanched almonds, coarsely chopped**

Preheat your oven to 400°.

Sift the first 4 ingredients together.

Stir in all your remainin' fixins', except the almonds, jest till moistened.

Fold in the almonds.

Fill paper-lined muffin tins full, and bake approximately 20 minutes.

Makes 12 muffins.

Apple Butter Muffins

In the early days when folks still made use of the cider press, Granny never failed to delight us with a batch of these moist, rich muffins every harvest season. We had quite a cold spell there last week, why, the old rooftop of John and Ellie's place looks a mite frostbitten. I must get on over to Creighton's apple orchard to gather up some windfalls, so's I can start up Granny's old press for my apple butter. And you know what kind of muffins the Jenkins will be treated to when they drop in on Wednesday.

2 cups flour
1 tablespoon bakin' powder
1/2 teaspoon salt
1 teaspoon cinnamon
2/3 cup sugar

1 egg, beaten
1/3 cup butter, melted
3/4 cup milk
1/2 cup apple butter

1 tablespoon grated orange rind
1 cup raisins

Preheat your oven to 400°.

Sift the first 5 ingredients together.

Stir in the egg, butter, milk and apple butter, jest till moistened.

Fold in your orange rind and raisins.

Fill paper-lined muffin tins full, and bake approximately 20 minutes.

Makes 12 muffins.

Ham Cheese Muffins

Down at the butcher shop some years past, that Norm Thompson tried to control his fool temper, but his efforts resulted in a drop of your temperature. That very icy fella, you see, had jest seen one of the Stokes hounds makin' off with his prize ham. And the results, a shortage of that spicy meat, which put me out in the cold for makin' any Ham Cheese Muffins for dinner that night.

- **2 cups flour**
- **1 tablespoon bakin' powder**
- **3/4 teaspoon salt**
- **1/4 teaspoon dry mustard**
- **2 tablespoons sugar**

- **1 egg, beaten**
- **1/3 cup butter, melted**
- **1 cup milk**

- **3/4 cup chopped ham**
- **3/4 cup grated Cheddar cheese**

Preheat your oven to 400°.

Sift the first 5 ingredients together.

Stir in the egg, butter and milk, jest till blended.

Fold in your ham and cheese.

Fill paper-lined muffin tins full, and bake approximately 20 minutes.

Makes 12 muffins.

Rum Raisin Muffins

All the folks are excited. They are jest bubblin' over. And do you know why it is? It's because they're fixin' all the goodies for the homecomin' picnic tomorrow. Matter of fact, I have a batch of very special muffins in the oven right this minute, full of plump raisins and laced with rum. This contribution to the book comes to you all, courtesy of our friends from New England. There's some that hold the New Englanders to be strait-laced. Isn't that a ring-tailed snorter of a thought for the day? These are nice for those festive occasions.

    1 cup raisins
    1 cup boilin' water
  1/4 cup dark rum

    2 cups flour
    1 tablespoon bakin' powder
  1/2 teaspoon salt
  2/3 cup sugar

    1 egg, beaten
  1/3 cup butter, melted

Pour boilin' water over raisins. Add rum and let set a spell. Thirty minutes should do it.

Preheat your oven to 400°.

Sift the flour with the next 3 ingredients.

Stir in your raisin mixture, the egg and butter, jest till moistened.

Fill paper-lined muffin tins full, and bake approximately 20 minutes.

Makes 12 muffins.

Concord Grape Muffins

My word, we used to laugh at Farmer Jesse. He still insisted on ridin' that fat black horse, Martha, who was harnessed to the roundabout. Now at that time, your automobile was jest comin' into existence. Of course, the old traditions die hard. One thing that Farmer Jesse was fond of doing, was fixin' up his homegrown grapes in these harvest treats.

 2 **cups flour**
 1 **tablespoon bakin' powder**
1/2 **teaspoon salt**
1/2 **cup sugar**

 1 **egg, beaten**
1/3 **cup butter, melted**
1/2 **cup sour cream**
1/2 **cup milk**

 12 **tablespoons grape preserves**

Preheat your oven to 400°.

Sift the first 4 ingredients together.

Stir in the egg, butter, sour cream and milk, jest till blended.

Fill paper-lined muffin tins 1/2 full.

Cover with 1 tablespoon preserves per muffin, then remainin' batter. Bake approximately 20 minutes.

Makes 12 muffins.

Harvest Carrot Muffins

In the old days, it was rare to see carrots put up in your average dessert. But these days, no baker worth his salt fails to bake up one of your delicious carrot cakes. Naturally, the homely veggie is equally at home in these spicy muffins, which are nice served up some bright October afternoon, when the folks drop in.

2 cups flour
1 tablespoon bakin' powder
1/2 teaspoon salt
1/2 teaspoon cinnamon
3/4 cup sugar

1 egg, beaten
2/3 cup milk
1/3 cup oil
1/3 cup crushed pineapple (in juice)

1/4 cup raisins
1/4 cup chopped nuts
1 cup grated carrots

Preheat your oven to 400°.

Sift the first 5 ingredients together.

Stir in the next 4 ingredients, jest till moistened.

Fold in the raisins, nuts and carrots.

Fill paper-lined muffin tins full, and bake approximately 20 minutes.

Makes 12 muffins.

Zucchini Nut Muffins

When the walnut tree is rainin' down nuts on the old roof, it's time to gather them all up to store away for the comin' cold season. In the old days, we would always set out on the annual nuttin' expedition to Murphy's Wood about this time. Don't you all miss out on the chance to try these Zucchini Nut Muffins which are moist and delicious.

- 2 cups flour
- 1 tablespoon bakin' powder
- 1/2 teaspoon salt
- 1 cup sugar
- 1/2 teaspoon ground cardamom
- 3/4 teaspoon cinnamon
- 1/4 teaspoon allspice

- 1 egg, beaten
- 1 cup milk
- 1/2 cup oil

- 1 cup grated, unpeeled zucchini
- 3/4 cup chopped dates
- 3/4 cup chopped walnuts

Preheat your oven to 400°.

Sift your first 7 ingredients together.

Add egg, milk and oil, and stir jest till blended.

Fold in your veggies, dates and nuts.

Fill paper-lined muffin tins full, and bake approximately 20 minutes.

Makes 12 muffins.

Potato Muffins

In the deep of the night when the screech owls are hootin', we sometimes hear the lonely whistle of the freight train headed north, with a cargo of our Irish potatoes. These muffins are cousin to the Sweet Potaty variety in this book.

1/3 cup butter, melted
1/3 cup sugar
  1 cup mashed, cooked potato
  1 egg, beaten
  2 cups flour
  1 tablespoon bakin' powder
3/4 teaspoon salt
  1 cup milk
3/4 cup raisins

Preheat your oven to 400°.

Combine your butter and sugar till smooth.

Stir in the mashed potato, then your egg.

Sift flour, bakin' powder and salt together.

Stir into the potato fixins', alternately with your milk.

Fold in the raisins.

Fill paper-lined muffin tins full, and bake approximately 20 minutes.

Makes 12 muffins.

Special Cornmeal Muffins

Many folks turn their noses up at the idea of eatin' your average cornmeal muffin. But would you risk a wonderful taste experience to listen to such bobcrackery. No sir, not when you try treats of Granny's, chock full of zesty currants and crunchy walnuts.

       1 egg, beaten
   1 1/2 cups milk
     2/3 cup brown sugar, packed
     1/3 cup butter, melted

       1 cup yellow cornmeal
       1 cup flour
       1 tablespoon bakin' powder
     3/4 teaspoon salt

     3/4 cup black currants
     3/4 cup chopped walnuts

Preheat your oven to 400°.

Sitr together the egg, milk, brown sugar and butter. Set aside a spell.

Sift together the cornmeal, flour, bakin' powder and salt.

Add the egg fixins', and stir jest till moistened.

Fold in your currants and nuts.

Fill paper-lined muffin tins full, and bake approximately 20 minutes.

Makes 12 muffins.

Applesauce Muffins

I reckon one of the most popular muffins in the old time Alabamy would be these Applesauce variety. My brother Steve, could polish off a plate of them while they were still having' a hot time coolin' off on the old windowsill.

2 cups flour
1 tablespoon bakin' powder
1/2 teaspoon salt
3/4 teaspoon cinnamon
2/3 cup sugar

1 egg, beaten
1/3 cup butter, melted
3/4 cup milk
1/2 cup applesauce

1/2 cup raisins

Preheat your oven to 400°.

Sift together the first 5 ingredients.

Add the egg, butter, milk and applesauce, and stir jest till moistened.

Fold in the raisins.

Fill paper-lined muffin tins full, and bake approximately 20 minutes.

Makes 12 muffins.

Chocolate Date Bran Muffins

Folks will talk about these Chocolate Date Bran Muffins for days afterwards. Don't bake them up if you have some of your unwanted houseguests. Jest might keep them hangin' 'round your doorstep till next year.

1 1/2 cups 100% bran cereal
1 1/2 cups milk
  1/2 cup whole-wheat flour
  1/2 cup all-purpose flour
    1 tablespoon bakin' powder
  1/2 teaspoon salt
  2/3 cup brown sugar, packed
    1 egg, beaten
  1/3 cup butter, melted
    1 cup chocolate chips
    1 cup pitted dates, chopped

Soak the bran in your milk for 15 minutes.

Preheat your oven to 400°.

Sift the next 5 ingredients together.

Stir in the egg and butter, jest till moistened.

Fold in your chocolate chips and dates.

Fill paper-lined muffin tins full, and bake approximately 20 minutes.

Makes 12 muffins.

Winter

Seem's like no time at all till Old Man Winter comes sneakin' up on you.

Now's the time to take advantage of your year round seasonals, such as bananas, and citrus fruits from our Floridy neighbors hard by. It's also a good time to stock up on herbs and spicys. These are useful for Sweet Potato Muffins, and many others in the muffin kin.

One day, my Granny told us, she was out shoppin' in the village, and was jest startin' back for home, when she notices this hoky little shack leanin' against a big, old warehouse. Well sir, in she goes and finds more herbs and spicys than you'd see in a lifetime. "Where in the Sam Hill do you get all these?" she asks. That sly little man, he jest grins like the backwater swamp where the 'gators are. "Here," says he, "lies a regular jackpot of those beneficient herbs."

Anyways, this is where we all get our bakin' necessities, but you folks can get them in any of your regular stores.

All told, I figger the best way to enjoy winter is to put your feet on the stove, and cozy up with a good book, while you're waitin' for your muffins to bake, and your kinfolk to come and help you eat them.

Nesselrode Muffins

Paul the fix-it man, baked this one up, one snowy day nearin' Christmas. He always laid claim that he couldn't boil water, but what's a mystery to me, is how he managed to bake up these delicious festive goodies off the top of his head.

   2 **cups flour**
   1 **tablespoon bakin' powder**
1/2 **teaspoon salt**
3/4 **cup sugar**

   1 **egg, beaten**
1/3 **cup butter, melted**
3/4 **cup cream**
1/4 **cup rum**

1/2 **cup shaved chocolate**
1/2 **cup candied fruits**
1/4 **cup raisins**

Preheat your oven to 400°.

Sift the first 4 ingredients together.

Stir in the egg, butter, cream and rum, jest till moistened.

Fold in the remainin' fixins'.

Fill paper-lined muffin tins full, and bake approximately 20 minutes.

Makes 12 muffins.

Chocolate Fudge Muffins

Here comes Granny's invention for those days when you need your real break. These Chocolate Fudge Muffins are rich and decadent, loaded with little chocolate nuggets, inside and out. As Daddy always said, they're good enough to bring a smile to the face of your most hardened sourpuss.

3/4 cup boilin' water
1 cup chocolate chips
1/4 cup butter

2 cups flour
1 tablespoon bakin' powder
1/2 teaspoon salt
1/2 cup sugar

1 egg, beaten
1/3 cup shortenin', melted
1/2 cup milk
1/2 cup sour cream

3/4 cup chopped walnuts

1/2 cup chocolate chips

Preheat your oven to 400°.

Combine your boilin' water, chocolate chips and butter, and melt over low heat, stirrin' constantly. Remove from the stove.

Sift the next 4 ingredients together.

Stir in the egg, shortenin', milk and sour cream, along with your chocolate fixins', jest till blended.

Fold in the walnuts.

Fill paper-lined muffin tins full, sprinkle with the chocolate chips, and bake approximately 20 minutes.

Makes 12 muffins.

Sesame Seed Muffins

One of your saucy little nuthatches is beggin' for vittles, out in the garden, hard by the smokehouse. I've seen the juncos around lately too, I guess they figgered they wanted the easy end of the stick as usual, and they didn't care too much for huntin' their meal themselves. I usually save one of my muffins for the birds, or if I have a nutty one, for the squirrels. 'Nuts for the squirrels', as Granny's sayin' went. Purty soon my Sesame Seed Muffins will be ready to pull out of the oven, which should suit my feathered friend out there jest fine. And it will be a perfect opportunity to have a welcomin' tea for the new folks, who jest moved in down the road.

2 cups flour
1 tablespoon bakin' powder
1/2 teaspoon salt
1 cup brown sugar, packed

1 egg, beaten
1/3 cup butter, melted
1 cup milk

2 teaspoons grated orange rind
1 teaspoon vanilla extract
3/4 cup sesame seeds

Preheat your oven to 400°.

Sift the first 4 ingredients together.

Stir in the egg, butter and milk, jest till moistened.

Fold in the remainin' fixins'.

Fill paper-lined muffin tins full, and bake approximately 20 minutes.

Makes 12 muffins.

Eggnog Muffins

I mind Christmas back when I was a girl. The old mill pond glowed from the bonfires cracklin' on the shores, and the air rang with the shouts of the young folk skatin' on the glassy ice. At that time of year, your eggnog was everywhere, mercy, it was all through the house. So it seemed to make sense to include it in these festive muffins, which became an annual specialty among our kin.

- 2 cups flour
- 1 tablespoon bakin' powder
- 1/2 teaspoon salt
- 2/3 cup sugar

- 1 egg, beaten
- 1/3 cup butter, melted
- 3/4 cup eggnog
- 1/4 cup rum

- 1/2 teaspoon nutmeg

Preheat your oven to 400°.

Sift the first 4 ingredients together.

Stir in the egg, butter, eggnog and rum, jest till blended.

Fill paper-lined muffin tins full.

Sprinkle with nutmeg, and bake approximately 20 minutes.

Makes 12 muffins.

Sunshine Bran Muffins

I guess the main reason why our local hermit kept to himself so much, was on accounta' his gigantic clan of critters. Mind you, Granny was fond of them, and can't say I could do without myself, but Pete went regular hogwild, with everything from 'possoms to 'gators. Guess folks didn't fancy stayin' around your local zoo. So Pete moved out. Fact is, if I saw him now, I wouldn't know him if I tripped over him. But he used to make mighty fine Sunshine Bran Muffins. Here's my version of that wonderful recipe.

1 1/2 cups 100% bran cereal
1 1/2 cups milk
  1/2 cup whole-wheat flour
  1/2 cup all-purpose flour
    1 tablespoon bakin' powder
  1/2 teaspoon salt
  2/3 cup brown sugar, packed
    1 egg, beaten
  1/3 cup oil
  3/4 cup chopped fresh orange, peeled
      and sectioned
  3/4 cup chopped fresh grapefruit, peeled
      and sectioned

Soak your bran in the milk for 15 minutes.

Preheat your oven to 400°.

Sift the next 5 ingredients together.

Stir in the egg and oil, jest till moistened.

Fold in your citrus fruits.

Fill paper-lined muffin tins full, and bake approximately 20 minutes.

Makes 12 muffins.

Apricot Nut Muffins

These muffins are a wonderful midwinter treat, served pipin' hot and slathered with butter. Uncle Bert went quite nutty over these. Oh land, he used to get everybody going, once he started laughing. 'Uncle Bert with the Big Laugh', we young 'uns used to call him. You all should find these Apricot Nut Muffins very refreshing with their touch of orange.

> 2 **cups flour**
> 1 **tablespoon bakin' powder**
> 1/2 **teaspoon salt**
> 2/3 **cup sugar**
>
> 1 **egg, beaten**
> 3/4 **cup orange juice**
> 1/4 **cup milk**
> 1/3 **cup butter, melted**
>
> 1 **tablespoon grated orange rind**
> 1 **cup chopped dried apricots**
> 1 **cup chopped walnuts**

Preheat your oven to 400°.

Sift together the first 4 ingredients.

Stir in the egg, juice, milk and butter, jest till blended.

Fold in the remainin' ingredients.

Fill paper-lined muffin tins full, and bake approximately 20 minutes.

Makes 12 muffins.

Orange Date Nut Muffins

You know, dates are a wonderful complement to many of your household fixins'. You take for instance, bananas. Now here's a couple more things that are good with dates while we're talkin' about it. Peaches are always nice, and right now I've jest found Granny's prized recipe for Orange Date Nut Muffins.

2 **cups flour**
1 **tablespoon bakin' powder**
1/2 **teaspoon salt**
2/3 **cup sugar**

1 **egg, beaten**
1/3 **cup butter, melted**
1 **cup milk**
1 **orange, grated. (Use fruit, juice and peel.)**
1 **cup chopped dates**
3/4 **cup chopped walnuts**

Preheat your oven to 400°.

Sift together the flour with your next 3 ingredients.

Stir in the egg, butter and milk, jest till blended.

Fold in the grated orange, then the dates and nuts.

Fill paper-lined muffin tins full, and bake approximately 20 minutes.

Makes 12 muffins.

Cranberry Nut Muffins

Here is a good way to use up those cranberries after you've made enough sauce for your Christmas turkey. Now going back to the subject of leftovers, it's mostly boggledbotch. You see, there's never anything you can't do better with a vittle the second time around, as Granny always said.

>   2 cups flour
>   1 tablespoon bakin' powder
>   3/4 teaspoon salt
>   1 cup sugar
>
>   1 egg, beaten
>   1/2 cup orange juice
>   1/2 cup milk
>   1/3 cup butter, melted
>
>   2 tablespoons grated orange peel
> 1 1/2 cups cranberries, halved
>   1/2 cup chopped pecans

Preheat your oven to 400°.

Sift together your first 4 ingredients.

Stir in, jest till moistened, the egg, juice, milk and butter.

Fold in the remainin' ingredients.

Fill paper-lined muffin tins full, and bake approximately 20 minutes.

Makes 12 muffins.

Currant Streusal Muffins

These muffins are nice served with a cup of your English style tea. They are tender and delicious, with jest a hint of tang, and as I said to Abby the other day, so naturally British that we could set ourselves up one of those genuine afternoon tea shops.

  2 cups flour
  1 tablespoon bakin' powder
1/2 teaspoon salt
1/2 cup sugar

  1 egg, beaten
1/2 cup milk
1/2 cup sour cream
1/3 cup butter, melted

  2 tablespoons candied citron
1 1/2 cups dried currants

Toppin'
1/2 cup sugar
1/3 cup flour
1/4 cup butter

Preheat your oven to 400°.

Sift the first 4 ingredients together.

Stir in the egg, milk, sour cream and butter, jest till moistened.

Fold in your citron and currants.

Mix the toppin' fixins' till crumbly.

Fill paper-lined muffin tins full with the batter, sprinkle with toppin', and bake approximately 20 minutes.

Makes 12 muffins.

Christmas Muffins

No point in bein' like your Ebenezer Scrooge when it comes to buyin' the fixins' for these Christmas Muffins. The overnight steepin' gives a flavor similar to that of your nutty fruitcake.

1/4 cup sherry
1/4 cup raisins
1/4 cup candied pineapple, finely chopped
1/4 cup chopped maraschino cherries
1/4 cup slivered almonds

2 cups flour
1 tablespoon bakin' powder
1/2 teaspoon salt
1/4 teaspoon allspice, ground
1/2 teaspoon cinnamon
1/2 cup sugar

1 egg, beaten
1/3 cup butter, melted
1 cup milk

Marinate your fruits and nuts in the sherry overnight. Be sure to keep them covered.

Preheat your oven to 400°.

Sift together the next 6 ingredients.

Stir in the egg, butter and milk, jest till blended.

Fold in your nutty fruit fixins'.

Fill paper-lined muffin tins full, and bake approximately 20 minutes.

Makes 12 muffins.

Jaffa Orange Muffins

We all used to rise early back in the old days, my brother and I especially, and so did my girl chum. It didn't matter what day of the week, we were always up with your birds. Mama didn't seem to mind, and it keened our appetites for Granny's delicious muffins, such as these luscious citrus charmers.

- 2 cups flour
- 1 tablespoon bakin' powder
- 1/2 teaspoon salt
- 2/3 cup sugar

- 1 egg, beaten
- 1 cup sour cream
- 1/3 cup butter, melted
- 1 teaspoon orange extract
- 3 tablespoons grated orange peel

- 1/2 cup chopped pecans

Preheat your oven to 400°.

Sift the first 4 ingredients together.

Stir in the remainin' ingredients, except for the pecans, jest till moistened.

Fold in your pecans.

Fill paper-lined muffin tins full, and bake approximately 20 minutes.

Makes 12 muffins.

Sausage Muffins

When Margie and George were courtin', Granny would set the copper kettle simmerin' for homemade soup to go with these tasty Sausage Muffins. Now that couple used to come by quite a bit in those days, because see, Margie's mama wasn't a big cook.

    2 **cups flour**
    1 **tablespoon bakin' powder**
3/4 **teaspoon salt**
    2 **tablespoons sugar**

    1 **egg, beaten**
1/3 **cup oil**
    1 **cup milk**

    6 **small sausage links, (3 ounces) cooked and chopped**

Preheat your oven to 400°.

Sift flour with your next 3 ingredients.

Stir in your egg, oil and milk, jest till blended.

Fold in the chopped sausage.

Fill paper-lined muffin tins full, and bake approximately 20 minutes.

Makes 12 muffins.

Cherry Streusal Muffins

When the 5:39 comes through every evening, Tom the conductor, always comes around, hopin' for a batch of his favorite muffins. When Tom shows up, I always greet him with a smile, along with these lavish cherry muffins, crowned off by a buttery-rich streusal toppin'.

- 2 cups flour
- 1 tablespoon bakin' powder
- 1/2 teaspoon salt
- 2/3 cup sugar

- 1 egg, beaten
- 1 cup milk
- 1/3 cup shortenin', melted

- 1 1/2 cups tinned red cherries, drained

- 1/2 cup flour
- 1/4 cup brown sugar, packed
- 1/4 cup butter

Preheat your oven to 400°.

Sift the first 4 ingredients together.

Stir in the egg, milk and shortenin', jest till blended.

Fill paper-lined muffin tins 1/2 full, cover with cherries, then remainin' batter.

Combine the remainin' fixins' till crumbly, sprinkle over muffins, and bake approximately 20 minutes.

Makes 12 muffins.

Pineapple Tangerine Muffins

These select muffins of sun-drenched pineapple and tangerine taste as good as they sound. Each Friday, Grandpa Martin used to drive his horse across the Burlingame Bridge from his home in Scratch Ankle, to visit Granny, and relish these sensational muffins.

1 1/2 **cups flour**
1/2 **cup wheat germ**
1 **tablespoon bakin' powder**
1/2 **teaspoon salt**

2/3 **cup milk**
1/4 **cup pineapple juice**
1/2 **cup honey**
1/3 **cup butter, melted**

1 **tablespoon grated tangerine peel**
1 **cup crushed pineapple, drained**

Preheat your oven to 400°.

Sift the first 4 ingredients together.

Stir in the milk, pineapple juice, honey and butter, jest till moistened.

Fold in the tangerine peel and pineapple.

Fill paper-lined muffin tins full, and bake approximately 20 minutes.

Makes 12 muffins.

Cheddar Onion Muffins

You've heard tell of your egg eatin' dog, but our Badger was an incurable muffin eater. Why, seem's like every time Granny baked up a batch of these cheese and onion goodies, that varmint would make off with them again. Serve these hot, while the cheese is still meltin'.

2 cups flour
1 tablespoon bakin' powder
1 teaspoon salt
1/2 teaspoon paprika
2 tablespoons sugar

1 egg, beaten
1/2 cup milk
1/2 cup sour cream
1/3 cup butter, melted
1 cup old Cheddar cheese, grated

1/2 cup finely chopped onion
1/4 cup fresh parsley, finely chopped

Preheat your oven to 400°.

Sift together the first 5 ingredients

Add your remainin' ingredients except the onion and parsley, and stir jest till blended.

Fold in the veggies.

Fill paper-lined muffin tins full, and bake approximately 20 minutes.

Makes 12 muffins.

Lemon Muffins

I mind it was the winter of '22 when we had the grippe sneakin' around. My Grandpa, he was very bad with it. "Well, I've got it and I've got it good," he said to Granny. So she fixed him up her special lemon brew, and he was smart as a cricket. And with all those lemons left over, there were plenty for Granny to treat us to these heavenly muffins.

2	**cups flour**
1	**tablespoon bakin' powder**
1/2	**teaspoon salt**
1/2	**cup sugar**
1	**egg, beaten**
1	**cup milk**
1/3	**cup butter, melted**
2	**tablespoons grated lemon peel**
1	**teaspoon lemon extract**
1/2	**cup chopped pecans**

Preheat your oven to 400°.

Sift the first 4 ingredients together.

Stir in the egg, milk and butter, jest till blended.

Fold in the lemon peel, lemon extract and pecans.

Fill paper-lined muffin tins full, and bake approximately 20 minutes.

Makes 12 muffins.

Banana Buttermilk Muffins

Although John is one of your picky eaters, he claims that Ellie bakes the best banana muffins this side of the Mississippi. When it came to these Banana Buttermilk Muffins, Ellie said she couldn't leave John alone with them for more than ten minutes, before they'd disappear.

2/3 cup sugar
1/2 cup butter, softened
  1 egg, beaten
  2 bananas, mashed
1/2 teaspoon vanilla extract
  2 cups flour
  1 tablespoon bakin' powder
1/2 teaspoon salt
3/4 cup buttermilk
3/4 cup chopped walnuts

Preheat your oven to 400°.

Cream sugar and butter together.

Beat in egg, bananas and vanilla extract.

Sift your flour, bakin' powder and salt together.

Add to banana fixins', alternately with your buttermilk, stirrin' jest till moistened.

Fold in your walnuts.

Fill paper-lined muffin tins full, and bake approximately 20 minutes.

Makes 12 muffins.

Date Nut Muffins

Now Granny's eyes were very sharp, and lookin' down the road, she could see a great deal. Indeed, Granny could find out most anything when she had a mind to. So that's how she reckoned something was bakin' up in the oven at Ellie's the day her Great Granny arrived. And that's how she was the first to discover Ellie's Date Nut Muffin recipe.

1 cup chopped dates
2/3 cup sugar

1/3 cup butter
1 cup boilin' water

2 cups flour
1 tablespoon bakin' powder
1/2 teaspoon salt

1 egg, beaten
2 teaspoons lemon juice
1 teaspoon grated lemon peel

1 cup chopped walnuts

Combine dates and sugar in bowl that is heatproof.

Add your butter to the boilin' water and pour over dates and sugar. Stir till the sugar dissolves, then cool to room temperature.

Preheat your oven to 400°.

Sift the flour with the bakin' powder and salt.

Stir in the egg, lemon juice, peel and date fixins', jest till moistened.

Fold in your walnuts.

Fill paper-lined muffin tins full, and bake approximately 20 minutes.

Makes 12 muffins.

Sweet Potato Muffins

If you mind Granny's Pumpkin Muffins, then you will have an idea of what these Sweet Potato Muffins taste like. If ever you have some yams left over from your dinner vittles, then jest remember these spicy muffins, and bake up a baker's dozen to delight your kin.

1/2 cup butter, softened
3/4 cup sugar

  1 cup sweet potatoes, cooked and mashed
  1 egg, beaten

  2 cups flour
  1 tablespoon bakin' powder
3/4 teaspoon salt
3/4 teaspoon cinnamon
1/4 teaspoon nutmeg

  1 cup milk

1/3 cup chopped pecans
1/4 cup raisins
1/2 teaspoon lemon extract

  2 tablespoons sugar
1/2 teaspoon cinnamon

Preheat your oven to 400°.

Cream butter and sugar together.

Stir in sweet potatoes and egg.

Sift the flour with the next 4 ingredients.

Stir in sweet potato fixins', along with milk, stirrin' jest till moistened.

Fold in the nuts, raisins and extract.

Fill paper-lined muffin tins full, sprinkle with combined sugar and cinnamon, and bake approximately 20 minutes.

Makes 12 muffins.

Ginger Rum Muffins

These pungent muffins have an unusual hot and sweet flavor. Served warm, with a scoop of vanilla ice cream, they're out of this world. Now one thing here, give a mind to that ginger, if you are like Granny, and like to peck away at the fixins' as you go along. That would be because those chunks of ginger are little powderkegs that are guaranteed to give you your hotlips.

> 2 cups flour
> 1 tablespoon bakin' powder
> 1/2 teaspoon salt
> 2/3 cup sugar
>
> 1 egg, beaten
> 1/3 cup butter, melted
> 3/4 cup milk
>
> 1/4 cup dark rum
> 1/3 cup chopped, preserved ginger

Preheat your oven to 400°.

Sift the first 4 ingredients together.

Stir in the egg, butter and milk, jest till blended.

Pour your rum over the ginger, then immediately fold into your batter. Do not marinate this, as the ginger and rum make for your potent brew! A chance meetin' of these flavours is all you need.

Fill paper-lined muffin tins full, and bake approximately 20 minutes.

Makes 12 muffins.

Buttermilk Currant Bran Muffins

I'll be doggoned if I can't find my raisins today. I don't think I've got any of your near-sightedness yet, but I'll take a run on over to Doc Jackson's tomorrow anyways. Meanwhile, I'll jest bake up some of my spicy Buttermilk Currant Bran Muffins.

1 1/2 cups 100% bran cereal
1 1/2 cups buttermilk
1/2 cup whole-wheat flour
1/2 cup all-purpose flour
1 tablespoon bakin' powder
1/2 teaspoon salt
1 teaspoon cinnamon
1/2 teaspoon nutmeg
2/3 cup brown sugar, packed
1 egg, beaten
1/3 cup oil
1 cup dried currants

Soak the bran in the buttermilk for 15 minutes.

Preheat your oven to 400°.

Sift the next 7 ingredients together.

Stir in the egg, oil and bran fixins', jest till blended.

Fold in your currants.

Fill paper-lined muffin tins full, and bake approximately 20 minutes.

Makes 12 muffins.

Orange Bran Muffins

Granny never stood for your so called breakfast skippers. But if you can't face your vittles at 7 a.m., one of these Orange Bran Muffins is guaranteed to convert you to that first meal of the day.

1 1/2 cups bran cereal (your 100% kind)
1 1/2 cups buttermilk

1 cup flour
1 tablespoon bakin' powder
1/2 teaspoon salt
1 teaspoon cinnamon
1/4 teaspoon nutmeg
1/3 cup brown sugar, packed

1/3 cup molasses
1 egg, beaten
1/3 cup oil

1/2 cup chopped dates
2 tablespoons grated orange rind

Soak your bran in the buttermilk for 15 minutes.

Preheat your oven to 400°.

Sift together the flour with the next 5 ingredients.

Stir in the molasses, egg and oil, jest till blended. Then fold in the remainin' fixins'.

Fill paper-lined muffin tins full, and bake approximately 20 minutes.

Makes 12 muffins.

Hearthside Muffins

Some dull November day, when it's getting dark early, a dozen of these hearthside muffins, with a delicious date and coconut toppin', is a number 1 pick up for your case of the blues.

1 1/2	**cups flour**
2	**teaspoons bakin' powder**
1/4	**teaspoon salt**
1/3	**cup sugar**
1	**egg, beaten**
1/4	**cup butter, melted**
3/4	**cup milk**
1/4	**cup chopped dates**
1/4	**cup coconut**
1/2	**cup brown sugar, packed**
1	**egg, beaten**

Preheat your oven to 400°.

Sift the first 4 ingredients together.

Stir in the egg, butter and milk, jest till blended.

Fill paper-lined muffin tins 2/3 full.

Mix the dates, coconut, brown sugar and egg together, till well combined. Cover your muffins with this toppin', and bake approximately 20 minutes.

Makes 12 muffins.

Mincemeat Muffins

I'm not sure how mincemeat became popular at Thanksgiving, but these muffins are well worth givin' thanks for. Come that big holiday in November, the visitin' kin will be bustlin' around exchangin' news and such, while they prepare that Thanksgiving dinner of your roast turkey and your mince pies. Not to forget Granny's mincemeat muffins, to enjoy by the fireside later on, with a cup of hot cinnamon cider.

        2 **cups flour**
        1 **tablespoon bakin' powder**
    1/2 **teaspoon salt**
    1/2 **cup sugar**

        1 **egg, beaten**
    1/3 **cup butter, melted**
    1/2 **cup sour cream**
    1/2 **cup milk**

        1 **cup mincemeat**

Preheat your oven to 400°.

Sift the first 4 ingredients together.

Stir in the egg, butter, sour cream and milk, jest till blended.

Fold in your mincemeat.

Fill paper-lined muffin tins full, and bake approximately 20 minutes.

Makes 12 muffins.

Butterscotch Chip Raisin Muffins

We only used to have these muffins once in a donkey's age. Granny's excuse was that if she baked them up too often, we might get addicted. Mind you, we could always count on them after one of your old-time sleigh rides. You know, jest lookin' out at the moon tonight has set my mind wanderin' back to those times, as we skimmed over the icy Bay of Quincy. Oh, we had a marvellous evenin', the cold air makin' no never mind, because see, we were all covered up by one of your buffalo rugs. Hot chocolate was always waitin' for us, along with your baker's dozen of these rare muffins.

- 2 cups flour
- 1 tablespoon bakin' powder
- 1/2 teaspoon salt
- 2/3 cup sugar

- 1 egg, beaten
- 1/3 cup shortenin', melted
- 1 cup milk

- 1 cup butterscotch chips
- 1 cup raisins

Preheat your oven to 400°.

Sift the first 4 ingredients together.

Stir in the egg, shortenin' and milk, jest till moistened.

Fold in your butterscotch chips and raisins.

Fill paper-lined muffin tins full, and bake approximately 20 minutes.

Makes 12 muffins.

Banana Bran Muffins

The Evans family lived on the other side of town, hard by Copple Hill, in a ramshackle old cabin. I'm sorry to say that Elsie was the only one that showed the slightest promise of amountin' to a row of pins. The fellas were idle, shiftless folks, always in a state of your debt. Elsie took up a job in the local bakery, and was known to turn out a mighty fine banana bran muffin.

1 1/2 cups bran cereal (your 100% kind)
1 1/2 cups buttermilk

   1 cup flour
   1 tablespoon bakin' powder
1/2 teaspoon salt
   1 teaspoon cinnamon
1/4 teaspoon nutmeg
2/3 cup sugar

   1 egg, beaten
1/3 cup oil

   1 banana, mashed

   1 banana, sliced thickly

Soak your bran in the buttermilk for 15 minutes.

Preheat your oven to 400°.

Sift together the flour with the next 5 ingredients.

Stir in the egg, oil and your cereal fixins', jest till moistened.

Fold in the mashed banana.

Fill paper-lined muffin tins full.

Put a banana slice on each muffin, and bake approximately 20 minutes.

Makes 12 muffins.

Linzer Muffins

If you mind your famous treat, the linzer torte, you will find these muffins kissin' cousin to that European dessert. I mind Aunt Cora, she picked up with some folks from the mountainous region of Austria. The next thing I knew, we were all bein' treated to her version of linzer torte, in the form of these unique muffins, most every Saturday, when she came around.

- 2 cups flour
- 1 tablespoon bakin' powder
- 1/2 teaspoon salt
- 1/2 teaspoon cinnamon
- 2/3 cup sugar

- 1 egg, beaten
- 1/3 cup butter, melted
- 1 cup milk

- 12 tablespoons raspberry jam
- 12 tablespoons ground almonds

Preheat your oven to 400°.

Sift the first 5 ingredients together.

Stir in the egg, butter and milk, jest till blended.

Fill paper-lined muffin tins 1/2 full, cover first with the jam, then the nuts. Fill tins with remainin' batter.

Bake approximately 20 minutes.

Makes 12 muffins.

Cashew Coconut Whole-Wheat Muffins

With those frosty days of January jest a hair away, it never made more sense to take advantage of your nutty winter crop, although these days, they can be dear. I've jest been down to the dry goods store, and land sakes, prices are risin', even in the sticks. But I always try to make these at least once every winter, on accounta' their bein' so good.

1 cup whole-wheat flour
1 cup all-purpose flour
1 tablespoon bakin' powder
1/2 teaspoon salt
2/3 cup brown sugar, packed

1 egg, beaten
1/3 cup oil
1 cup milk

2/3 cup cashews, chopped
2/3 cup coconut flakes

Preheat your oven to 400°.

Sift the first 5 ingredients together.

Stir in the egg, oil and milk, jest till blended.

Fold in your cashews and coconut.

Fill paper-lined muffin tins full, and bake approximately 20 minutes.

Makes 12 muffins.

Apricot Bran Muffins

Dang it, if my Apricot Bran Muffins haven't jest come up nicely, and look who's comin' down the road but that Isabel Turner - again! Better run on out and say a Hello to the old gossip, hopin' in the meantime that these Apricot Bran Muffins don't burn. I don't want to lose that delicious batch, packed with sunny apricots from Californy.

1 1/2 cups 100% bran cereal
1 1/2 cups milk

1/2 cup whole-wheat flour
1/2 cup all-purpose flour
1 tablespoon bakin' powder
1/2 teaspoon salt
2/3 cup brown sugar, packed

1 egg, beaten
1/3 cup oil

1 1/2 cups finely chopped, dried apricots

Soak the cereal in the milk for 15 minutes.

Preheat your oven to 400°.

Sift together the next 5 ingredients.

Stir in the egg and oil, jest till blended.

Fold in your apricots.

Fill paper-lined muffin tins full, and bake approximately 20 minutes.

Makes 12 muffins.

Cranapple Wheat-Germ Muffins

*There's a lotta talk nowadays 'bout all them natural foods and livin'
off the land concepts. But folks these days thinkin' all this is new,
sakes, I've been makin' use of it since I was a girl back in Alabamy.
Now here's a fine example of one of your naturally nutritious muffins
that Granny used to bake up, with the added bonus of wheat germ.*

1 1/2 cups 100% bran cereal
1 1/2 cups milk
  1/2 cup whole-wheat flour
  1/2 cup all-purpose flour
    1 tablespoon bakin' powder
  1/2 teaspoon salt
  2/3 cup brown sugar, packed
    1 egg, beaten
  1/3 cup oil
    1 cup finely chopped apple, peeled and cored
  2/3 cup cranberries
  1/4 cup wheat-germ

Soak your bran in the milk for 15 minutes.

Preheat your oven to 400°.

Sift the next 5 fixins' together.

Stir in the egg and oil, jest till moistened.

Fold in the apple and cranberries.

Fill paper-lined muffin tins full, sprinkle with your wheatgerm and
bake approximately 20 minutes.

Makes 12 muffins.

Prune Streusal Muffins

We often used to have these Prune Streusal Muffins when the Potters dropped in. They were good souls; there was Emma, who insisted on bringin' her famous chicken soup around when any of us were sick. I daresay, there really is something to our old tradition of that hearty brew, and it's medicinal properties. Anyways, I think you all should enjoy these moist muffins, made especially nice with a buttery streusal toppin'.

2 cups flour
1 tablespoon bakin' powder
1/2 teaspoon salt
1/2 cup brown sugar, packed

1 egg, beaten
1/3 cup butter, melted
1 cup milk

2 teaspoons lemon peel
1 1/2 cups chopped, pitted prunes

1/2 cup brown sugar, packed
1/2 cup flour
2 tablespoons butter

Preheat your oven to 400°.

Sift the first 4 ingredients together.

Stir in the egg, butter and milk, jest till blended.

Fold in the lemon peel and prunes.

Mix your brown sugar and flour together. Cut in the butter till crumbly.

Fill paper-lined muffin tins full with your batter.

Sprinkle toppin' over, and bake approximately 20 minutes.

Makes 12 muffins.

Fig Rum Muffins

The Weaver hillbillies across the county line vie with our kin when it comes to makin' muffins. Now you take your average Weaver, she doesn't mind talkin' about bakin', but she's not going to tell anybody her recipes. When it comes to that, she's no loose lipper, she'll clam up like your small mouthed snapper. So here you have our version of the Weaver's recipe. You can use your prunes if you like, but we're kinda partial to figs.

- 1 cup dried figs, finely chopped
- 1/2 cup sugar
- 1/3 cup oil
- 1/2 teaspoon salt
- 1 cup orange juice
- 2 cups flour
- 1 tablespoon bakin' powder
- 1 egg, beaten
- 2 tablespoons dark Jamaican rum
- 2 teaspoons grated orange rind
- 1/2 cup chopped walnuts

Combine your figs with the next 3 ingredients.

Add the orange juice.

Preheat your oven to 400°.

Sift the flour and bakin' powder together.

Stir in the fig mixture.

Add the egg to these fixins'.

Fold in the remainin' ingredients, stirrin' jest till moistened.

Fill paper-lined muffin tins full, and bake approximately 20 minutes.

Makes 12 muffins.

Honey Spice Muffins

I mind one winter when we young 'uns took it into our heads to walk over to Aunt Sally's on our own. Now she lived way out at Three Forks, oh, it must have been six miles or more. We walked for ages, and then the doggoned snow started up. We never did get there. When we finally found our way back home, Granny was waitin' for us with hot water bottles, mugs of steamin' hot chocolate, and a dozen of these Honey Spice Muffins.

- 2 cups flour
- 1 tablespoon bakin' powder
- 1/2 teaspoon salt
- 1/2 teaspoon cinnamon
- 1/4 teaspoon allspice
  dash ground cloves and nutmeg

- 1 egg, beaten
- 1/3 cup butter, melted
- 3/4 cup milk

- 1/4 cup boilin' water
- 1 tablespoon instant coffee powder
- 1 cup liquid honey

Preheat your oven to 400°.

Sift the first 6 ingredients together.

Stir in the egg, butter and milk, jest till blended.

Dissolve the coffee in your boilin' water. Stir this, along with the honey, into your batter.

Fill paper-lined muffins tins full, and bake approximately 20 minutes.

Makes 12 muffins.

Index